SEPTEMBER '03

DEAR DAVID,

HAPPY BIRTHDAY!

DON'T GO THE SAME WAY AS SYD NOW YOU'VE REACHED 40.

Love + Kisses

The Greys

x

madcap

madcap

the half-life of Syd Barrett, Pink Floyd's lost genius

TIM WILLIS

* SHORT BOOKS

First published in 2002 by
Short Books
15 Highbury Terrace
London N5 1UP

10 9 8 7 6 5 4 3 2 1

A CIP catalogue record for this book
is available from the British Library.

ISBN 1-904095-24-0

Printed in Great Britain by
Mackays, Chatham, Kent

AMDG

‘There was Syd Barrett with his white face and his black eyeliner all round his eyes – this strange presence, singing in front of a band that was using light shows. I thought, “Wow! He’s a bohemian, a poet, and he’s in a rock band!” ’

David Bowie has a career epiphany at the Marquee Club, 1966

‘I’m full of dust and guitars’

Barrett in 1971

CONTENTS

Brief Encounter (A)

THE received wisdom is that you don't disturb him. The last interview he gave was in 1971, and from then until now, there are only about 20 recorded encounters of any kind. His family says it upsets him to discuss the days when he was the spirit of psychedelia, beautiful Syd Barrett, the leader of Pink Floyd. He doesn't recognise himself as the artist responsible for that band's classic first album; nor as the shambling visionary who, during an extended nervous breakdown exacerbated by his drug intake, made two solo LPs which are as eternally eloquent as Van Gogh's cornfields. He doesn't answer to his Sixties nickname now. He's called Roger Barrett, as he was born in 1946.

On a blistering hot day, pacing the cracked tarmac pavement in this suburban Cambridge street, I wonder if I can act honourably by him. 'He doesn't recognise himself' implies a disability. But might Barrett not, by a mental trick, have refused to recognise his time as the musician Syd – and have abandoned that identity? The pain of those associations might be avoided if he could rediscover himself as young Roger, the eccentric schoolboy, the brilliant young artist.

When the DJ Nicky Horne doorstepped him in the Eighties, Barrett said, 'Syd can't talk to you now.' Perhaps, in his own way, he was telling the truth. But I could talk to him as Roger; ask him if he was still painting, as reported. I could pass on regards from friends he knew before he became 'Syd'.

Two housewives in the street say he ignores their Good Mornings when he goes out to buy his *Daily Mail* and changing brands of fags. 'He's always in a singlet and shorts, summer and winter. He doesn't seem to feel the cold.'

On his bike or on foot, Barrett stares straight ahead. Apart from his sister, they don't think he has any visitors – not even workmen. But they don't see why I shouldn't take my chances. It's been a few years since backpackers camped by his gate. 'He didn't open the door for them, and he probably won't for you.'

So I walk up the concrete path of his grey pebbledash semi, try the bell, and discover that it's disconnected. At the front of the house, all the curtains – blue, patterned, double-lined – are open. The side passage is closed to prying eyes by a high plank gate. I knock on the solid front door and, after a minute or two, look through the downstairs bay window. Where you might expect a television and a three-piece suite, Barrett has constructed a bare, white-walled workshop. Pushed against the window is a dusty, tattered pink sofa. On the scored hardboard tops, toolboxes are neatly stacked, flexes coiled, pens put away in a white mug.

Then, a sound in the hall. Has he come in from the shady back garden? (It must stretch for 60 feet.) Perhaps it needs mowing, like the front lawn – although, judging by the mound of weeds by the path, he's been tidying the beds today.

I knock again, and hear three heavy steps. The door flies open, and he's standing there.

He's stark naked except for a small, tight pair of bright blue Y-fronts; bouncing, like the books say he always did, on the balls of his feet.

Some of his biographers claim that the skinny, impish

dandy has become a fat old man. But, paunch apart, Barrett is in good shape, more muscular than you'd imagine, sweating a little, his teeth slightly bared. His balding head is shaved very close. The only reminders of his corkscrew perm are a few dark hairs that straggle down his neck. He bars the doorway, with one hand on the jamb, the other on the catch. His resemblance to Aleister Crowley in his Cefalu period is uncanny; his stare about as welcoming...

Foreword

In 1988, the *News of the World* quoted the writer Jonathan Meades, recalling an incident from 20 years before. Meades had visited a South Kensington flat shared by Barrett with a bright, druggie clique from Cambridge. 'This rather weird, exotic and mildly famous creature was living in this flat with these people who to some extent were pimping off him, both professionally and privately,' said Meades. 'There was this terrible noise. It sounded like the heating pipes shaking. I said "What's that?" and [they] sort of giggled and said, "That's Syd having a bad trip. We put him in the linen cupboard." '

It's a common motif in the Barrett legend: the genius mistreated, forced to endure unspeakable mental anguish for the fun of his fairweather friends. But it's not necessarily true. There are some terrible tales from that flat in

Egerton Court. But on this particular occasion, as flatmate Aubrey 'Po' Powell remembers it, 'Pete Townshend used to come there, and Mick and Marianne. It was an incredibly cool scene. Jonty Meades was a hanger-on, a straight cat just out of school. I'm sure we told him that version of events – but only to wind him up.'

Similarly, Barrett's lover and flatmate at the time, Lindsay Corner, denies the stories that he locked her in her room for three days, feeding her biscuits under the door, then smashed a guitar over her head. This time, however, three other residents swear he did: 'I remember pulling Syd off her,' says Po. And that's the trouble with the whole Barrett business. There are witness accounts by people who weren't there, those who were there disagree – and are prone to constant revisionism – and half of them, being as totally off their faces as Barrett was, must have a question-mark over their evidence. If you can remember the Sixties, as they say…

Look at 101 Cromwell Road, another Barrett address from that decade. This now-demolished building has gained a reputation as either the Seventh Circle or Shangri-la. Some visitors recall the groovy 'happenings' in '65, with Jagger and Ginsberg and the Lennons calling on the Cambridge hipsters Nigel and Jenny Lesmoir-Gordon in the ground-floor flat. Others describe the top maisonette, where Barrett lived two years later, as 'the biggest shit-heap, a total acid shell', and home to 'acid-in-the-reservoir, change-the-face-of-the-world, acid missionaries'. Here, according to the biographies, you were scared to drink the tap water in case the cold tank had been spiked. But, really, how wild could either place be when the first floor housed the Katinka School of Dance, and the second a teacher called Berty Poliblanc, who pulled out the fuses when things got too rowdy?

Trying to pin Barrett down, you can feel like Henry Thoreau chasing the loon bird on Walden pond: every time you row to where the loon last dived, it pops up 50 yards behind you, cackling madly. But journalists have also muddied the waters. At the end of the Sixties, once rumours of Barrett's 'madness' spread, some used the cheap trick of quoting his conversation syllable for syllable – which would make anyone sound certifiable. Others failed to realise that Barrett was making them look ridiculous, adopting a Dylanesque attitude to interviews. The result is that reports of Barrett's life (and death, in a shop doorway, according to *Sounds* in 1986) have been wildly exaggerated.

It has been estimated, for example, that in '67 he took upwards of 200 acid trips. Yet Alistair 'Jock' Findlay, who lived with Barrett in Cromwell Road for a few weeks, says that he took much more than his mildly famous friend; and Jock puts his own tally for that year at 15. For acid to have been the cause of Barrett's breakdown, one would expect him to have had at least one bad trip. No one specifically remembers him having one – though Jock says he went a bit wobbly when Lindsay Corner nail-varnished two cockroaches pink.

His schedule certainly speaks against him constantly tripping. Forget writing, rehearsing and broadcasting. In '67 – on top of the photo-shoots and interviews, business and band meetings – Barrett made nearly 200 concert appearances in America, Europe and Britain, and had about 60 sessions in the studio (often on the night shift). Sometimes, he and his band would play two different countries in the same day. Roger Waters, who was in Pink Floyd with him and shared that incredibly hectic period, claims that he never saw Barrett tripping at a gig or in a studio.

But hang on. Though Waters may now say that LSD

was 'emphatically not' at the root of Barrett's mental problems, in the Sixties he was equally emphatic that his colleague had 'overdosed on acid'. And Jock's girlfriend Sue Kingsford – with whom Barrett had been a student at Cambridge Tech – claims that they took LSD together 'most days' that year.

We're back with our contradictory witnesses. But this is the big unanswered question about Barrett's breakdown. How much were drugs to blame? The various LSD theories will be dealt with later (frequency and flashbacks, strength and spiking). And one should note here that Barrett was a fanatical dope-smoker – day and night, year in, year out – which can be dangerous for the mentally delicate. But it's worth remembering that, when someone has a genetic predisposition to such illness, it can be hard to tell what exactly triggers it, which exactly is the back-breaking straw. And then, of course, madness may be just acting out of context. And who's to say what the right context and actions are?

It's all a bit baffling and – to make matters more difficult – the confusion was probably stoked by Barrett himself. In homage to the vogueish psychology of RD Laing, was he flirting with schizophrenia? The musician

Daevid Allen says of the insane glaring that accompanied his breakdown: 'It was very fashionable for everyone to sit around with staring eyes, like everyone was demented.' The artist Duggie Fields, who shared a flat with him in the early Seventies, says that the notorious photographs of a gaunt, unshaven Barrett, with matted hair and haunted aspect, actually conform to a post-hippie 'grunge' look, popular at the time – 'although they *were* taken on a particularly bad hair day'.

After Barrett's behaviour had ruined Pink Floyd's first American tour in '67, he turned up at the office of his first love, Libby Gausden, 'dressed in a green velour sweater and tight green trousers. He said, "Is it me, or is it a blade of grass?" He knew he'd been very naughty in America – that's what he called it – but he was joking about it. He wasn't at all mad.' Anthony Stern, a college chum, remembers that at the height of his aberrance, the well-read Barrett enthusiastically discussed Hamlet's 'antic disposition'. 'Syd was always acting,' he says. 'Who knows how much?' Many people have remarked that it was hard to tell whether Barrett – the child or the man, sane or not – was laughing at them. ('He might have looked through people,' says one, 'but he saw right through them, too.') And on top of that, as David Gilmour – his old friend and replacement in Pink Floyd – points out, a mental illness needn't disable the whole mind: 'Just because one part of someone's brain goes wrong, that doesn't mean the rest does. Even at his most bonkers, Syd was still incredibly clever.'

All this would be immaterial had Barrett not been such a great artist, a painter of soundscapes, a performer of pictures, a poet with the potential to rival Dylan – or indeed, Keats. Without artifice, even his fey accent was a work of art, later imitated by David Bowie and Marc Bolan.* Whether or not Barrett had Nabokov's gift of synaesthesia, his aim was to engage the mind's eye as well as the ear – and to appeal directly to the feelings with works that were not so much songs as mood pieces.

Peter Jenner, his co-manager with Andrew King, remembers how the 20-year-old Barrett 'drew' them, like Venn diagrams. Rado Klose (known by his second name of Robert, or 'Bob') recalls that, when they played guitar together in an early version of Pink Floyd, Barrett

* Bolan was so in awe of Barrett that he asked to be taken on by the same management in '67. Not only did he adopt Barrett's perm and make-up, he also married the management's factotum, June Child.

once heard a C chord, and said: 'That's yellow.'

When Barrett became the Floyd's electric lead, his style was experimental, to put it mildly. ('His instrument was the equipment, not the guitar,' reckons Klose.) From his late teens, he had been playing with controlled feedback – rolling ball-bearings down the neck, sliding over the strings with a Zippo lighter, detuning and retuning while he performed. The effects – blips and screeches and howls – would be fed through foot-operated echo units, making wave upon wave of sound on which to skim his licks. To this day, only David Gilmour knows how he made that rhythmic, scratching slap on his 'cat song', 'Lucifer Sam'.

In the early gigs of Barrett's Floyd – flailing ghosts among the light-shows, slides and films – they played formless jams, waiting to happen on the right groove. But on record Barrett created a crystalline world, bringing alive the bookshelves of a clever middle-class schoolboy: the *Alice* adventures and Fenland folk tales; Grahame's riverbank sagas and Lear's nonsense; Eng. Lit. texts, Tolkien, comics and esoteric religious pamphlets.

He could make a song out of anything – out of his laundry list or his mental condition – and it always reflected the latter. He shared a joint with an impressionable fan and wrote 'See Emily Play'. He heard about a knicker fetishist raiding the washing-line of Roger Waters' mum, and came up with 'Arnold Layne'. He would pop his later lovers into his Floyd lyrics: Jenny Spires in 'Lucifer Sam' ('Jennifer Gentle, she's a witch'); or Lindsay Corner in 'Apples and Oranges' ('Cornering neatly, she trips up sweetly'). However, even before he went solo, he was changing direction, becoming less figurative and more abstract.

The best pieces of his later period – in fact, his best pieces, period* – were sloppily played on an acoustic guitar, the words picked for their sounds and associations, to make a backing track to his own troubles and an epitaph for the woeful naivety of the summers of love. He once had a girlfriend called Viv Brans, nicknamed 'Twig'. In 'Dark Globe' – a title pinched from *The Lord of the Rings* – he sings: 'The poppy birds sway,/ Sing Twigs coffee Brans around.' What does it mean? What does it

* Apart from the author's favourite, 'No Man's Land', on the first solo album, *The Madcap Laughs*. Anticipating fuzz-metal, this track also features an immortal, barely audible third verse. Hearing his mutterings on playback, Barrett preferred the achieved effect to clarity, and left it alone.

matter? You can *feel* the melancholy. You can hear the fear in 'Baby Lemonade': 'In the sad town/Cold iron hands clap/The party of clowns outside.'

But he was more than a naive talent. 'Lucifer Sam' is surely a nod to Christopher Smart's poem *Jubilate*, with 'my cat Geoffry'. And take the shanty-phrase from 'Octopus': 'The madcap laughed at the man on the border/ Hey ho, Huff the Talbot.' Huff, of course, is the nursery-rhyme dog, co-star with My Cat Tib. He represents Lord Talbot who, in Shakespeare's *Henry VI*, describes himself as the 'public spectacle... the scarecrow that affrights our children so'. And 'Scarecrow' is a sad track from the Floyd's first album, *Piper at the Gates of Dawn* – which phrase itself is an image from *The Wind in the Willows*. Barrett has an obvious appeal to the trainspotting wing of rock'n'roll.

One of the Great Barrett Lines Of All Time is from the Floyd's second LP, to which he hardly contributed. It comes at the end of the album, after a cacophonous section on 'Jugband Blues'. A frail voice emerges, with a faintly strummed accompaniment. 'And what exactly is a dream?' he asks. 'And what exactly is a joke?' Jenner described the song as 'a portrait of a nervous breakdown'

– and it is. But as Barrett once said, *pace* William Empson, 'I think it's good if a song has more than one meaning.' 'Jugband' is also an exercise in sarcasm and an attack on his colleagues, ultimately questioning the worth of wanting to be a rock star. To Barrett's mind, becoming one wasn't up to much. And it's his mind that makes his music so fascinating.

True, he would be less intriguing had he stayed in the public eye. But that combination of dramatic past and unfulfilled potential began a cult, which grew when his old band became superstars. The Floyd's memorial to him, 'Shine On You Crazy Diamond', fanned the legend's flame in the Seventies, as did the true story that Barrett had turned up at Abbey Road studios while his ex-colleagues were tinkering with the track in question. The boys hadn't recognised him at first, because he had grown enormously fat.

Pink Floyd's drummer Nick Mason has likened Barrett to James Dean. Other rock stars who fried their brains and died have been invoked – Hendrix, Joplin, Morrison, Jones, Cobain. But another synaesthetic, the poet-turned-gunrunner Arthur Rimbaud, has been a better comparison. Rimbaud and Barrett both started new lives, leaving images of themselves which, unlike their contemporaries', would never age. Barrett is like Shakespeare in his Stratford retirement, a hero turned Everyman. And more potent yet, though this metaphor for the hippie dream is still very much alive, he won't comment on his myth.

You can comprehend the scale of his cult by visiting the Internet: key 'Syd Barrett' into the Google search engine, and you'll be directed to 32,000 sites. But don't expect too much enlightenment. I once registered with a 'web ring' where Barrettomanes correspond. Four hours later, I had to de-register, having received over 40 emails, mostly debating whether or not he secretly played on the Beatles' *Sergeant Pepper*.

Well, he didn't – of that I'm certain. And, though I do not pretend to omniscience about Barrett, I can at least promise more accuracy than has previously been achieved. I am particularly hopeful that the spelling of names and the sequence of events are finally correct in this account. And at least fantasies and mistakes have been weeded out; primary sources re-interviewed, or sometimes questioned for the first time. There is still a wealth of material to be uncovered by researchers more assiduous than me – but if you can't find any well-known Barrett tale here, then it probably didn't happen, or is too trivial to mention.

One further point: the sexual mores of Barrett's generation – and particularly of the man himself – differed widely from today's. Notions of fidelity were somewhat elastic. To give an idea of them, I have hereafter divided his partners into 'girlfriends' and 'serious girlfriends', his relationships into 'affairs' and 'serious affairs'. Normally, from the age of 15 to 24, he was simultaneously involved in at least one of each – as, sometimes, were the girls themselves.

Madcap

MOST of the people in this story had well-off, academic parents from Cambridge and its environs. Born on 6 January 1946, the fourth of five children, Roger Barrett was no exception. Dr Arthur 'Max' Barrett was a pathologist, the university's Morbid Anatomist. His wife Winifred had been in catering. Disciples of Baden-Powell, they met on top of a haystack during a scouting outing in 1930, and married five years later. Max was 26, Win was 31. In 1949, after the birth of their fifth child Rosemary, they moved to one of the five-bedroomed, double-fronted houses on Cambridge's southern approach road. It had a huge, light entrance hall, and the side staircase opened on to a wooden gallery around the first floor.

At 183 Hills Road, Win kept the 100-foot garden in splendid condition. A regular pillar of the community, she ran an old folks' lunch club and was a high-up in the county Guides. Her husband pursued his amateur interests: painting watercolours in the nearby Botanical Gardens, to which he had a private key; and collecting mushrooms and fungi, which he described and illustrated for publication. He also belonged to the Cambridge Philharmonic Society – and enjoyed a family singsong round the old upright in the music room.

Roger Barrett's eldest brother, Alan, was born in 1937, followed by Donald and Ruth (who later moved away from Cambridge). Alan, Roger and Rosemary still live within a short drive of each other: 'Rog' and 'Roe' have remained particularly close, while Alan looks after his brother's business affairs. The eldest three children have been described as rather distant figures, but they seem to have been tolerant of their kid brother's antics – tearing through the house with lit sparklers and the like. In later life, Barrett had fond memories of birthdays, 'with their parties and games that you play in the dark, when someone hides and hits you with a cushion. We also used to dress up and go into the street and throw stones at passing cars.'

He once dropped a rubber plant, to see if it would

bounce. From birth until the age of 21, he charmed and amused anyone who ever met him. He drew incredibly well – but then, he did anything well, if it interested him. Aged seven, he won a piano prize at the Cambridge Guildhall, for playing a duet of 'The Blue Danube' with Roe (and then gave up the piano). Roe and he slept in the same bedroom for a while: 'After the light was turned out, he would sit up and start conducting an imaginary orchestra. The music was in his head, even then.'

When he was frustrated in his wishes, Barrett could throw terrible fits. According to one of his old teachers, he was sometimes a reluctant pupil, who needed to be walked by Max to the Morley Memorial Junior School down the road. But Roe has told friends that they 'loved' skipping off together, hand in hand. And any shyness had certainly vanished by grammar school. After passing his 11-plus and entering the County, also in Hills Road, he effortlessly took the lead in plays, and won public-speaking and poetry competitions. He developed an extraordinary facility with words, filling a page of his Boots' A4 diary every day. Puns, jokes and ambiguities poured out of him (and explain his liking for *The Goons*, Wilfred Pickles and, later, *That Was The Week That*

Was). But, like his literary hero Edward Lear, he loved painting above all else. Barrett was selling work (but refusing commissions) from the age of 14. His school-friend John Gordon has often told how Barrett would nick off cross-country runs and race home for an hour with his easel.

Music, for the moment, came a close second. With Radio Luxembourg under his pillow, he would listen out for Lonnie Donegan's 'Rock Island Line'. As skiffle bands became the national craze – his brother Alan played sax in one – Barrett took up the ukulele. But he was never quite like everybody else. When Elvis mania arrived, he preferred to concentrate on the banjo. He only appreciated rock'n'roll as it offered the weirder riffs of Bo Diddley, or the echo-fests of Buddy Holly and the Shadows. Aged 14, he begged his parents for a guitar – a £12 Hofner acoustic – and began jamming in his bedroom with John Gordon.

Barrett greased his hair into a quiff and tried to be a Ted, but he couldn't help being different. In the end, he hit on a Left Bank Existentialist image: shades, black drainpipes, a sloppy sweater and – a first for Cambridge – grey moccasins. (Otherwise, he preferred to go laceless and sockless, which was more comfortable for his wide, flat feet.) Hanging out at a trad-jazz club, he befriended the house band, whose drummer was one Sid Barrett – and these jazz cats called him 'Syd with a y' to differentiate him.

'Syd the Beat' – the nickname began to stick at school, and Barrett liked the Goonishness of 'Syd-Knee' and 'Sydernee'. However, with his first serious girlfriend, Libby Gausden, he generally referred to himself in letters and conversation as 'Rog' from '61 until at least '64. Apart, that is, from the times when he signed himself 'Roger Keith Barrett, Schoolboy' – or decided that his sobriquet should be 'The Baron'.

In turn-of-the-Fifties Cambridge, each teenage school-year produced about 200 girls and boys on the scene, of whom about 20 or 30 were cool to varying degrees. Of these, the coolest two or three were taken up by the coolest in the year ahead – and even in the year ahead of that, if they were super-cool. As they grew older, some stayed at school for 'A' Level exams, others continued at colleges of further education, others found work. At 18, a few went on to take degrees, though rarely in their hometown, and their absence was filled by incoming undergraduates. From 14 onwards, most were trying the drugs *du jour*. In 1960, speed could still be bought over the chemist's counter, and dope became available from about '62. But the real gear-change came with the arrival from the States of LSD-25 in 1963.

Twenty years before, Dr Albert Hoffman had taken history's first acid trip while trying to find a cure for asthma. In the intervening decades, news of the drug's effects – and huge batches from Hoffman's Swiss laboratory – had found their way to the Beat circles in New York. The British cultural attaché Michael Hollingshead kept a mayonnaise jarful in his fridge, in pure liquid form, and his parties in the early Sixties have achieved iconic status. Carefully dispensing drops on to sugar-cubes, he was the first to turn on Aldous Huxley and the future acid guru Timothy Leary.

According to John 'Hoppy' Hopkins – who was one of London's original hippies – there was among Hollingshead's acquaintance a nameless Cambridge chemistry graduate, on a research grant at Stanford University. This character returned to Britain with not only some of Hollingshead's batch – but also the formula! Enterprising students at Cambridge's world-renowned laboratories were soon manufacturing LSD. And as a result, until it was outlawed in 1965, acid consumption was more widespread in this small Fenland town than in all but the most exclusive circles in the capital.

Various shifting alliances developed in Cambridge's hip one hundred. Whizzing round on push-bikes, they met at Miller's music emporium, or on the riverbanks and meadows which creep almost to the ancient city centre. They hung out in coffee bars, pubs and dance halls, the homes of lenient parents, and the flats of those scenesters lucky enough to rent their own. But their sights were set on London, only 90 minutes away by train, lift or hitch.

By the beginning of the Sixties, the capital had started to swing. The broken, blitzed city was rising again in concrete and glass. Post-war rationing had been consigned to oblivion, and conscription was soon to follow. Adam Faith and Cliff Richards, Helene Cordet and Alma Cogan – they'd never had it so good: driving E-Types, drinking at the Saddle Room and dancing the Hully-Gully. Colin MacInnes had discovered the front line in Notting Hill, and Peter Cook had started *Private Eye*. Tony Armstrong-Jones was taking pictures for

Queen magazine, and (let's not forget huge social changes) the Pill went on sale.

In this second jazz age, the intelligentsia again turned to America for ideas. Poets like Michael Horovitz and Peter Brown spread the gospel of Ginsberg, who inspired the beginnings of an underground press and the opening of the 'alternative' Better Books in Charing Cross Road. Art-school figures, like Hornsey's Mike Leonard, tried to develop the light-shows first attempted by the darkly Beat writer William Burroughs. Most of the Cambridge crowd aspired to join one of the disparate scenes now emerging in London. When they succeeded, in the middle of the decade, they still kept in close touch.

***

The connections ran deep. When Barrett was six, he had attended the same Saturday-morning art club as David Gilmour and Roger Waters, at Homerton teacher-training college, again on Hills Road. By his teens, the cool network looked like this: a couple of months younger than County-boy Barrett, Gilmour was at the Perse, a Common-Entrance private school, once again on Hills

Road. Two years above them at the Perse were Anthony Stern, Seamus O'Connell and David Gale (who will all reappear in this story).

A year above them at the County were Storm Thorgerson, later Pink Floyd's art director, with and without Po, and Bob Klose, whose family were firm friends with Gilmour's. Waters was a year above those two, along with his best friend Andrew Rawlinson, and a year above him was his mate Geoff Mottlow, a fully fledged rocker by 1960 – and a future member of the Boston Crabs. At the university were Peter Jenner and Sam Hutt (later doctor to the Floyd scene, and, later still, known as the performer Hank Wangford), both of whom were familiars of the wannabe film director Nigel Lesmoir-Gordon and his future wife Jenny.

Waters, Klose and Thorgerson were in the County cricket team together; Waters, Mottlow and Rawlinson in the rugby team. Meanwhile, Waters' mother taught at Barrett's primary school, and Thorgerson's mother taught Lindsay Corner art at nearby Ely girls' grammar, where Po was two years above her in the boys' section. Lindsay's father, a botany professor, went mushrooming with Max, and Libby Gausden's father taught at the Tech (where Barrett, Gilmour and John Gordon would study). The Waters family lived round the corner from the Barretts, though in more straitened circumstances; the Gausdens were a few houses up Hills Road; and all the mums were close friends.

In 1961, there were three significant events in Barrett's life which affected each of these people to some degree. In June, he asked out Libby Gausden – a serious relationship which lasted, on and off, for about three years. At about the same time, he bought his first electric guitar, a Futurama 2, for which he built his own box-amp. And in December, his father died of cancer in hospital, after weeks in pain. Max's death made Barrett the young master of his domain. Until then, he had his own bedroom upstairs and shared a 'playroom' to the right of the front door. Now he moved his life into the ground-floor, front-left room, which was fitted with his own Yale lock. The older children had all left home, so Win began to take paying guests – two to each spare room.

Many middle-class families in Cambridge still take well-to-do lodgers. In the case of Roger Waters' widowed mother Mary, they were a financial necessity. For the Barretts', they were gilt on the gingerbread.

'Picasso's son Claude, who was at a language school, was with a family in the area,' says Libby Gausden, 'and we had a couple of Kuwaiti princesses with us. Their rents paid for our foreign holidays.' No 183 Hills Road lodged, among others, Japan's current prime minister Junichiro Koizumi, Jeanne Moreau's daughter and a future British duchess. The Barretts didn't do 'abroad' themselves. But, apart from foreign holidays, Win's smallest boy wanted for nothing.

Always indulged, he was positively spoiled now. Tea trolleys were left outside the door for him and his intimates. He made Win laugh so much that, when he was rude, she'd only say, 'You are a one!' When he started smoking, she said, 'Don't you think that's silly, dear?' Bob Klose came round to learn teach-yourself Pete Seeger tunes from Barrett ('Syd had the Seeger record'), who also practised them with David Gilmour ('Dave had the Seeger book, too'). The room was a chaos of clothes, guitars, paints. But, remembers Po, 'hanging from the ceiling – and I always thought this was a good metaphor for Syd's mind – were three delicate, beautifully constructed tetrahedrons that he'd made from balsawood. The calm eye of the storm.'

A storm indeed. No 183 Hills Road became base for the first band that Barrett was in: Geoff Mott and the Mottoes (founded by Mottlow). Roger Waters, who was learning the bass, sometimes joined their practices. Other times, he took Barrett out for terrifying rides on his new motorcycle, 'a 1946 Francis Barnet 125, that I'd bought with pea-picking money'. With Barrett on rhythm, the Mottoes played competent R'n'B at a few parties but had only one ticketed public performance, covering Eddie Cochrane numbers at a local CND fundraiser. Despite a duffel-coated fan base, the band broke up soon after. Waters went to study architecture at Regent Street Poly in London – where Klose would follow him – while Barrett went to the Cambridge Tech before starting at Camberwell School of Art. In the holidays, they hatched plans to form a new group, once they were all up in the smoke. Waters remembers how, on a train ride up to town, he and Barrett sketched a plan of how to put three guitars and a mike through two small amps.

Barrett began setting some words to music: James Joyce's poem 'Golden Hair'; another called 'The Effervescing Elephant', based on the verse of Lear and Belloc. (One minute and 175 words long, this ingeniously silly song's lyrics leave no room for breath, are sublimely rhymed, and have a truly bathetic ending.) None the less, he still presumed that he would be a painter.

It has often been alleged that Barrett was profoundly unsettled by Max's death. Also, that a bond consequently existed between him and Waters, who had lost his own father on the beaches of Anzio when he was one. Barrett's diary entry for 11 December was certainly only four words – 'Poor Dad died today' – but Waters doesn't remember them sharing any grief. Gausden says that 'Rog was more upset that his father had been in pain; that's what puzzled him.' And, having seen the ream of letters from Barrett that Gausden has saved, Gilmour says: 'I used to think that Syd's troubles were rooted in issues about his parents. Now I think he went through a period of sadness and then got on with his life.'

The very first letter Gausden has from Barrett is a semi-formal reply to her condolences over Max's death: 'I could write a book about his merits,' says Barrett. 'Perhaps I will sometime.' But he ends on a less sombre question about a recent gift: 'PS: What did you do with the necklace effort?'

***

At the Cambridge girls' grammar, fashion demanded a Germanic, chocolate-box look in June 1961: blonde pigtails with Shetland jumpers and skirts. Larking around on the Sheeps Green seesaw – her dark hair cut within two inches of her scalp and her knickers still wet from swimming – 15-year-old Libby Gausden did not conform. Like Barrett, who was passing the outdoor pool that day, she had a style of her own. 'They should put *you* on a Dairy Box,' he said. On their first date, they took a rowing-boat on the river. 'He was hopeless,' chuckles Libby. 'Hilarious. And that's what kept us together – we were always laughing.'

Barrett enjoyed life to the full. From drama summer-schools in Winchester, or scouting and sailing on the Norfolk Broads, his letters to Libby bubbled with mirth. Sometimes, even from home, he wrote twice a week. If he couldn't find paper, he used the backs of old envelopes, covering them with expert drawings and cartoons, riddles and nonsense stories. Youth has notorious energy, but Barrett seems to have filled his every waking hour.

The letters to his 'little Lib' sometimes run to thousands of words apiece.

One describes – with illustrations – how he hadn't enjoyed his mum's curry and had dropped the plate, which the cat had licked, so he killed the cat and buried it. (It ends with a depiction of a coffin with a curled tail.) Another is written in baby-language and script – 'There once was a girl called Elisabeth who lived in a house' – but accompanied by a meticulous architectural floor-plan of the building. Another, cut out of newspaper letters in 'blackmailer' style, anticipates the designer Jamie Reid's work for the Sex Pistols by decades: 'As you can see, I've got time to waste!'

Then there's the cute love-letter with Libby's imagined reactions on a separate sheet. ('I do, darling – oh yes, very marvellous, I'm sure... well, I like that!') Or the fantastically detailed and captioned drawing of himself waiting for a hot bath to cool down. Or the strip cartoon of a stick-girl and boy, forever coming together and parting until they hold hands and have a thought-bubble of babies. Then there's the poems: 'I love Lib./It's not a fib/ That I love Lib/Ad Lib Ad Lib Ad Lib.' And: 'Roasted chickin,/Honey thighs,/I'll love Lib/ Until I dies./But I yam old/And Lib is wise,/And also she has got nice eyes/And also she has got nice lips and feet (Blank verse).'

Gausden was privy to all Barrett's thoughts: how he liked reading – yawn – *On the Road*, or what his favourite hits were. Bed-bound with glandular fever, he writes: 'The Big Ben Twist' is the ultimate. I really rave over that one. (Jim Saville remark!) And it's in fashion. I *must* be ill.' He calls her 'Dwarling' when he's feeling affected, and 'Jezebel' when he's feeling jealous of her other boyfriends, John Swain – or 'John Swine', as Barrett dubs him – and a rival artist from the County, Dave Gilbert.

The letters are unremittingly passionate. Some are witty: 'I'm in bed. I'm in love. Only wish I could add "with you" to the first as well as the second.' Some are smutty. Some are full of tortured euphemisms pleading his lust and cursing Libby's father for his part in frustrating it. 'That's why I'm getting rougher,' he says – so his anger at being thwarted had clearly not diminished. However, by '62, he was able to remark chirpily: 'Funny about that French letter business, wasn't it?'

Gausden's *billets-doux* are a remarkable cache. Sydologists will be astounded to learn that by '64, Barrett had already written 'Let's Roll Another One', as well as two songs called 'Butterfly' and 'Remember Me' – or that Waters had penned a number called 'Walk With Me, Sydney'.* They will be intrigued when Barrett writes: 'Don't think I'm one of those people who say they'll be rich and famous one day.' They will smile at his turn of phrase – when he has a cold, he is 'very dying and almost dead' – or at his drawing: 'A Retch Goez to School With his Paints in a Box While All Sleep and Are Not Bothered'.

He is always an entertaining correspondent. Unusually bored while scouting in Suffolk, he writes: 'There are ladybirds on the Dunwich cliffs lying so thick on the ground that it's impossible to step without killing at least one. It's horrible to hear the crunch under your feet, and I wish I were dead.' Before matriculating for his Camberwell course, he reports: 'I have got an interview

* Contrary to any previous reports, this was Waters' first-ever song, the jokey but spookily prescient lyrics written for Barrett and Juliet Gale [see page 56]. Gale: 'Oooh, walk with me, Sydney.' Barrett: 'I'd love to love to love to, baby, you know.' G: 'Oooh, walk with me, Sydney.' B: 'I'd love to love to love to…' G: 'Ooh Sydney, it's a dark night./ Hold me hold me hold me hold me hold me hold me tight.' B: 'I'd love to love to love to./ But I've got flat feet and fallen arches, baggy knees and a broken frame./ Meningitis, peritonitis, DTs and a washed-out brain.'

tomorrow or Wednesday, so I only hope they accept me. Otherwise, I believe plumbing is a very steady job.'

Sometimes, he's hilarious: 'I have walked around looking at those little cards in windows advertising rooms to let. Trouble is, I don't want to live with horrid "NO COLOUREDS PLEASE" people, but all the others say "Coloureds Welcome", and I feel a meany depriving them of a room, so I'm worse off than them!' Sometimes he's less generous to minorities. On a party invitation that he designed at the time – to 'Bo Siddley's Perverted Bleach Party' – he couldn't resist adding: 'No pooves'.

The last two letters (with this author's punctuation) are among the most poignant. In the first he describes his first London lodgings, 'in the heart of beatland', and makes an unfortunate joke about drugs: 'Here I am Lib, in my little room, very warm, sitting on a blue blanket on a woolly bed on a cold leather couch, looking out of the window, listening to Radio London… The fire is on all day because the meter is broke. So it is very snug here, too, if you want Lib… Today I painted a picture of a duck (still) and a junkie. Had your black bomber [amphetamine pill] yet? They're the first step to the big H, Lib! (Said so on the telly).' The second is from '65, a baby-come-back letter, to which he has added a page in a deliberately 'mad' scrawl: 'You're so bloody stupid. I give you love and you refuse. You're bloody daft.'

Barrett and Gausden were forever breaking up and making up. 'In the end,' she says, 'we went out together because he thought I was someone that I wasn't, and I wanted him to be someone that he wasn't.' One could tell it from their clothes. Libby aspired to being a Bond Street Mod. Barrett was a Beat. In '63, when Win took Gausden, Roe and Barrett on the bizarre treat of a short break at Skegness Butlin's – to make up for no holiday the year before, following Max's death – Libby managed to force him into a skinny suit and narrow tie. ('That only lasted three days.') She even stopped him from bouncing for a while. But, more in character, 'He would threaten to dump me if I came out in my pink Chanel suit.'

Her father might have been relieved if Barrett had. Mr Gausden was distinctly quizzical of this strange boy, prancing around sockless, in laceless, shapeless shoes. Was he hopped up? Would Libby be smoking pot next? Actually, no. And though she knows Barrett took drugs, she can't remember him doing so with her. What she does remember is his magnetism. How he was chatted up by Mick Jagger when they went to watch the Stones at Whittesley in '63; and by the fashion designers Mary Quant and Barbara 'Biba' Hulanicki when they met at a Dylan concert in the Festival Hall. How, when he came to study in London, they visited the Tower and the Zoo (which Barrett had loved since childhood visits and where he had a special affection for Guy the Gorilla); or endlessly returned to a film about the Tokyo Olympics, which he loved for its 'naughty bits'.

Barrett had the silliest sense of humour: 'He cracked up when he saw a blind-crossing sign: "I mean, how are they meant to see it?"' He had the oddest quirks: 'He liked us to wash each other's hair until it was squeaky-clean.' And he approached the world from a unique angle: 'For example, he adored names. He wanted a bike called the Pink Witch – a girl's bike, really – and when he got one, he always referred to it by its full name of "the Pink Witch".' Gausden was impressed by his acting abilities at school (in Pinter and Beckett, *The Caucasian Chalk Circle* and *She Stoops to Conquer*) and by his prowess as a portraitist. But she couldn't bear it when he grooved to Miles Davis and Ray Charles; she was dubious when he dropped figurative for abstract art, 'man', and started working fabric and lace into canvas; and she just couldn't get him to be like the suave John Swine.

'We were always falling out over his presents. I'd want "Ferry 'Cross the Mersey" and he'd bring me "Red Bird". Once, he gave me a red candle and a blue-glass fisherman's ball. Another time, he gave me a strange twisted pottery sculpture – I still use it as a doorstop. Then there's an abstract painting of his called "Red Nativity" – he changed the title to "Little Red Rooster" after about two years. [It comprises uninspiring splotches of various reds-on-red.] And a big blue thing, for which I chucked him, one Christmas.' Barrett said, 'You're so *mean*. I thought you'd love it.'

When he started at Camberwell, Gausden came up from Cambridge one weekend and he went down the next. They had some holidays at home, too. But she was becoming disenchanted by Barrett's scene, if not the man himself. 'I thought psychedelia was ridiculous, superficial, and I preferred my own type of superficiality. I sometimes wondered why he was taking those wankers so seriously. But even when he was surrounded by weirdos, he was always pleased to see me. He always behaved like the old Rog with me.'

As part of her modern languages course, Gausden went to Germany for a year in 1965, and was engaged when she saw Barrett again, two years after that. But she remembers some of the Floyd's earliest gigs. ('Even then, the girls were screaming, "Syd! Syd!", which made Roger Waters very grumpy. He'd say: "We're not the bloody Beatles."') And Barrett remembered her in the 'Love Trilogy' on *Madcap*. Looking back, Gausden says: 'I never knew he was as gorgeous as he was. I think he hankered after everything being simple, but it all got so complicated so quickly. In the end, I think I was a bit of sanity in the madness around him.'

But we're getting ahead of ourselves. Back at the Cambridge Tech, in the winter of '62, Barrett was a restless pupil. He wanted to paint – here! now! – not to attend lectures on plaster-casting. He pretended to be physically deformed and, prophetically, mentally disturbed to unnerve boring teachers; and disconcerted them by strumming his bare toes over the Hofner beneath his desk. He remained keen on the guitar, buying a bass. (Libby remembers the tedious hours he spent practising.) He still played at parties, briefly joining a cover band called the Hollerin' Blues. He practised at college with John Gordon. But he was no technical match for Gilmour, also at the Tech and, for his part, supposedly studying for 'A' Levels in modern languages.

At lunch-breaks, aspirant guitarists met in the art department to teach each other the latest hit singles, often gleaned from quick listens in the booths at Miller's. Barrett and Gilmour would swap licks, and work out duets. Once or twice on summer evenings, they took their guitars down to a favourite hang-out of the scene, the Mill Pond, next to Queen's College, where they serenaded their friends. But Gilmour's musical ambitions were more focused than Barrett's. The next year, he became a semi-professional, then professional singer-guitarist, eventually teaming up with John Gordon and some ex-Mottoes in Jokers Wild, a top-notch dance band covering the Four Seasons and the Beach Boys.

If Gilmour was the more skilled musician, he was only Barrett's equal in the drugs department. Both were discovering the wonders of LSD, magic mushrooms and hash. 'But there was a seriousness to acid then, and even to dope,' says Gilmour. 'We wanted to explore the subconscious reaches of the mind, untap its potential. We were trying to understand the universe.' And to have some fun along the way. Friends of Storm Thorgerson could expect to be coerced into the comic shorts he made with his cine-camera: dressing up as nannies and babies to push each other in prams around the Fens; hanging upside-down naked; having a picnic where the meal was the other guests.

But Cambridge was getting too small for Barrett. He even skipped a local Beatles gig to attend his interview at Camberwell. (He borrowed a pair of Mr Gausden's lace-ups.) And in May '64, he and Anthony Stern held a joint exhibition of paintings in a room above the Lion and Lamb pub, in the commuter village of Milton. As Stern remembers it, 'the business of being avant-garde was too important for us to worry about selling anything', but the local paper's review contradicts him. Stern's efforts were indeed pretty appalling, with cactussy-fingery things set among coloured cut-out triangles. Barrett's figurative portraits and landscapes – drawings, prints and monotypes – were described as 'slight' and 'necessary student exercises', but the reviewer was gracious enough to allow that he was 'a sensitive handler of oil paint'.

According to the nimble-fingered Bob Klose, 'Syd could only strum E and A major, and a twelve-bar blues, but he could bloody paint.' As well as his skill, Barrett brought 'an incredibly decisive attitude' to his art (which Klose also noticed in the Floyd's early recordings). 'I'd be laboriously sketching a bridge, or a church, when Syd would walk by. He'd pull out his pad, go scribble-scribble, and it'd be finished, beautifully. You know – "That's what you want to do. Now, come on, let's get a coffee."' Klose seems to remember that bikes figured large in Barrett's work for the Milton exhibition, and that he sold one picture. Stern sold none and says: 'It was a dispiriting, downbeat event.' Later to become a swinging assistant and director, he adds: 'I think it's what turned me away from painting and into film. I don't know if it affected Syd the same way.'

***

By the summer of 1964, Seamus O'Connell and his bohemian mother had moved to the West End of London, where they rented a decrepit flat in Tottenham Street. Barrett found a bedsit in the same block, which he shared that autumn with David Gale. The latter, who had taken a year out from Cambridge University and found a job at Better Books, recalls: 'It was a terrifying building, with Irish navvies having drunken fights and screams in the middle of the night.' Po – by now resident in Cambridge and sharing a notoriously druggie flat – claims that once, when he was visiting Tottenham Street, he lifted the lid on a bucket and found a miscarried foetus inside.

Gale's memories are less macabre: yet more visits to the Zoo, where Barrett sketched a baboon picking its bum and eating it; and a celebrity-spotting game: 'You'd get six points for Petula Clark, five for Sandie Shaw.' (Barrett sent a portrait of Shaw to her management, but never heard back.) The boys hung out with Mrs O'Connell, who read their palms and taught them about tarot and the *I-Ching*, and they kept in touch with old mates. After one weekend in Cambridge, Barrett returned with his right eye looking deader than his left. Perhaps he had suffered a brain trauma; he claimed to have had a mystical encounter with Nature. But then, he enjoyed saying hippie-dippy things like that, playing up to the 'wows' of his credulous admirers.

Back in Cambridge, Andrew Rawlinson was running 'happenings' in the Round Church. As a project, he traced all the countries of the world from an atlas, cut them out and sent them to his circle, asking that they should be decorated and returned to him: 'The idea was an unpredictable group creation.' Barrett got Russia and coloured it light blue. When Rawlinson sent him an artefact made from *Marvel* comic cut-outs, Barrett sent back a booklet called *Fart Enjoy*.

This recently resurfaced work is a holy relic in Syd studies. Twelve sides of A4 taped on to brown card, a mixture of collage and typescript, it was the product of two nights' work and must be one of his earliest attempts at the cut-up method made popular by William Burroughs – and again borrowed by Bowie. The title, one assumes, was chosen for its sound, reminiscent of (Com)fort and Joy. The next page is inspired by RD Laing's trendy phrase, 'divided self', and is no doubt very exciting to Barrett scholars, though it only consists of thesaurus definitions of both words, split in two and typed above a face torn from a magazine, itself staring out of a painted, cracked egg. Barrett has added a speech-bubble in pen: 'Hallo!'

Next is a page with doodles on it. 'Add a mark,' says Barrett in 'blackmailer' letters. Then a cut-out text culled, it appears, from fashion and pop magazines, the Bible and other books. ('...Thus says the Lord God sex symbol good made death unto me? Dank corridors hear pop entries ashamed in this same confident boasting mortal blown knobbly slabs of white stone rubble...') But three particular pages stand out. A copy of a pedestrian letter to 'Roge' from Win, which may have been faked by Barrett. ('How did the group get on at Essex? I gather Don can't afford you?') A clever conjoining of a wildflower guide, Beatrix Potter's *Jeremy Fisher,* and a scientific text on pond life. And the letters of 'Boys Fuck Girls', typed in various combinations and juxtaposed with a picture of a porno model, on which Barrett has drawn and written childish obscenities – such as 'Fuk Suk and Lik' on the girl's lips.

At art school, there was enough room for painting and music in his life. So, almost immediately, Barrett hooked up with Waters and Klose to pursue the plans for a band. In fact, the pair had started without him. At Regent Street Poly, Waters had joined various other students to form Sigma 6 – also known as the Architectural and the Screaming Abdabs, the Abdabs pure and simple, the Meggadeaths and the T-Set – and had played some college dances. By the time Barrett arrived, they were the Spectrum Five. The musicians comprised Waters on bass, Klose on guitar, and two London boys from Waters' year on drums and keyboards – respectively, Nick Mason (still in today's Pink Floyd) and Rick Wright (likewise). As vocalist, they recruited Chris Dennis, an RAF dental technician from Cambridge, lately of the semi-pro Redcaps and owner of a good PA system. Also Juliet Gale, an 'A' Level student at the Poly who would later marry Wright, occasionally guested and sang backing.

'What am I going to do?' wailed Barrett, when he first heard them practise. 'Play rhythm and replace Chris,' answered Waters. For although Dennis, 26, had a big repertoire of blues numbers by heart, he also had the habit of closing numbers with Hitler impersonations, using his mouth-organ as a moustache. Luckily, he was posted to the Gulf before he could be fired. Barrett bought a white Fender Esquire, and later adorned it with round mirrors. Surprisingly, he was a reluctant frontman, unconvinced by his vocal powers. Klose thinks that 'Syd only managed by devising strategies. He had to act the part.' And a friend's comments hadn't helped, Barrett wrote to Libby: 'He says why don't I give up 'cos it sounds horrible, and he's right and I would, but I can't get Fred to join because he's got a group. So I still have to sing.'

This letter actually rewrites the history of Pink Floyd – since 'Fred' was the Cambridge nickname of David Gilmour (at the time, in Jokers Wild). If nothing else, Barrett's remark proves that he had mooted the recruitment of Gilmour long before the rest of the Floyd. And though Mason, Waters and Wright have no recollection of Barrett suggesting this, it must be possible that he planted the seeds of a plan which they later cultivated.

Whatever, that year most of the new band passed through the north London house of the Hornsey lecturer Mike Leonard. He had met Waters at one of the Poly's architectural functions, and announced that he had two shared rooms to let in the basement of his Highgate house. By the New Year, Mason and Wright had been and gone – back to their parents – and the lodgers comprised, in one room, Klose and Dave Gilbert, Barrett's old rival in love and art; and in the other, Waters and Barrett. Meanwhile, David Gale moved to a purple-doored pad in Earlham Street, on the corner of Cambridge Circus, which – like the groovy Lesmoir-

Gordons' new place in Cromwell Road – was a city-centre rendezvous for Cambridge exiles. These people could act cool to the point of freezing – but Mason remembers Barrett being exceptionally friendly, then crossing the room to greet strangers with a smile. Waters has a different recollection: 'Syd would often give a theatrical shudder and say: "Ugh! *People*!" '

Mike Leonard adored him. Here was a kid as happening as the light-machines that he was making for Hornsey's Light and Sound Workshop – which themselves were becoming integral to the underground scene. At first, in Leonard's hands and others', these devices had smacked of Heath-Robinson: old projectors with revolving discs attached, the discs being decorated with patterns, objects and coloured cellophane. But soon flashing lights and strobes joined them, along with superimposed pieces of film, and trippy, organic oil-slides – their bubbles expanding, bursting and reforming. (These last were made by using an upended projector to 'cook' coloured ink on oil-covered slides, then reflecting the projection on to a wall or – as was later the case with Pink Floyd – band.)

The lodgings in Stanhope Gardens became a finishing

school for Barrett and Waters. Thirtysomething Leonard gave them the run of his house, letting them practise on his piano, rehearse in his attic, read his progressive books, borrow his sidereal atlas. He soon had the synaesthetic Barrett wondering how to combine lights and music. Moonlighting in the advertising industry, he also owned a library of wacky sound-effects, which interested the boys. It was here that Barrett began to write in earnest, and to develop the distinctive Floyd sound with Wright – the only properly trained musician among them – who was about to transfer to music college.

At first, however, the Spectrum Five were a pub band with ambitions. They offered their services to the Woodman around the corner, and received £10 a night. They appeared at student parties. They played along to Leonard's lights at a few Hornsey workshops – where Klose felt rather lost and Barrett freaked out in his element. Through friends of friends, they found a brief residency at the Countdown Club in Knightsbridge. One night, back in Cambridge – after a frantic dash to the Musicians' Union office to get their cards – they were welcomed as heroes at Homerton.

Answering adverts for auditions in the music press,

they were turned down as support house group at Beat City in Oxford Street, and for the TV show *Ready Steady Go!*. Without success, they entered a couple of band contests. And some time in the spring, Barrett came up with the group's name. Though he later told dolly-bird journalists that he'd received an alien communication – 'wow' – in fact, he combined the names of two old Delta bluesmen, Pink Anderson and Floyd Council. The joke goes that they could have ended up as Anderson Council.*

There were plenty of laughs in that house – and no acid. Leonard would feed his cat by nailing a kipper to the wall. When it was Barrett's turn on the rota to cook Sunday lunch, he served up whole cabbages, and nothing else, because he thought the budget was for them all, not per person. By May, the lads had blown most of their grants on equipment and an old white Bedford van, on the bonnet of which Barrett daubed the band's name in pink and black paint. A friend of Wright's wangled them a free afternoon in a recording studio and they put four songs on tape, of which two survive as bootlegs. The

* Actually, a Pink Floyd tribute band now performs under this name.

chunky 'Lucy Leave', by Barrett, owes much to the Beatles' and Stones' sounds of the day. 'King Bee' is almost indistinguishable from the later Stones' version of Slim Harpo's classic. The third track is unknown, and the fourth was Diddley's 'Double-O Bo'. 'The title was the only reason for doing that one,' says Klose.

The light-shows, the sound-effect solos, the lateral thinking, the nuttiness of Barrett's new 'Bike' song – none of this really washed with the jazz-blues purist Klose, who was also worried that his studies were slipping, so he left the band amicably at the end of the academic year. However, his departure presented the Floyd with a problem: none of them could play very well. 'It was the making of Syd,' says Klose now. 'He was the frontman and it was his band. Faced with his technical limitations, he had to say: I can't do this, so I'll do that.' But *that* could wait until after the holidays.

An eventful three months followed. Back in Cambridge without Libby, Barrett began a serious affair with the gorgeous Lindsay Corner; they went sketching together, near Fulbourne psychiatric hospital – a building he would come to know well. He hooked up with Nigel Lesmoir-Gordon, also in town for the summer, and 'starred' in his rather dull home-movie* about a group of short-haired freaks from Cambridge taking magic mushrooms in a derelict quarry. (Later marketed as *Syd's First Trip* – which it wasn't – in it, the director, who was also on mushrooms, watches a self-conscious Barrett running around the lip of the quarry, marvelling at a butterfly on a leaf, being transfixed by the age-rings in a log, holding his hands up to the sun, and finally posing as a 'vegetable man' with field mushrooms over his eyelids and mouth.) But his biggest adventure in that summer of '65 was to take a lift with some old classmates to St Tropez, meeting up at a campsite with David Gilmour, who had gone on ahead.

Altogether, they spent a fortnight in the south of France. Barrett, as he always would, refused sunscreen and blistered terribly. Gilmour taught him songs from the Beatles' newly-released *Help!*, and together they tried to busk in the quayside tourist area. Unaware that they needed a performer's licence, they were picked up by two gendarmes and put in the cells for a few minutes. 'But the

* To stop its circulation, David Gilmour subsequently bought the rights to this shoddy film when it was released on video. However, it is still widely available on the Internet.

best times,' recalls Gilmour, 'were on the way back. We dawdled along, and Syd was always playing word-games with the road signs: "We've been too long" he'd say for Toulon, or "No time to lose" for Toulouse. It was busy in Besiers, nice in Nice, and so on.'

They camped for nearly a week outside Paris. One day, Barrett and Gilmour went to the Louvre, where 'Syd was like my personal guide – he knew all about everything'. Another day, they trawled the Left Bank stalls for Olympia Press books – banned in Britain – and bought *The Story of* O and *Naked Lunch*; in their tent by torchlight, the pair read them aloud. In September, Gilmour carried on in Cambridge with Jokers Wild, while Barrett took Corner to London. About to enrol in the Lucy Clayton modelling school, Corner sat at the rear of the train. Barrett sat up front, to avoid her father.

***

Many more cool Cantabrigians moved to London in late '65, and a game of musical flats ensued. Waters, on his way to living with his fiancée in Shepherd's Bush, spent a few weeks in the seven-bedroomed upstairs maisonette at Cromwell Road, where he knew Duggie Fields, a fellow architecture student from the Poly, and the ex-Tech girl Sue Kingsford. As in university digs, it had a pay-phone in the hall, almost sealed-over with the wax from dripping candles. Says Fields: 'A student sense of hygiene prevailed.'

Po and Thorgerson set up with David Gale and others a 10-minute walk away in the Egerton Court pad, which they decorated in bright blocks of colour. Barrett took the attic in Earlham Street where, among a rotating cast of pals from home, he had two firm friends in Peter Wynne-Wilson and his girlfriend Susie Gawler-Wright, also known as 'the Psychedelic Debutante'. (Wynne-Wilson, whose hobby was making 'cosmonocles' – prisms welded on to spectacles – later became a Floyd lighting-man.)

Before collecting Corner from Cambridge, Barrett had acquired a cat called Rover and done his room up with shawls and beads, rush matting, an easel and a double mattress at one end. 'Very artistically, he used a brown paper-bag as a lampshade,' remembers Po. 'Incredibly cool.' American imports were prominent in his record collection – the Mothers of Invention, the

Right: Barrett with chimp at London Zoo, 1952

Below: Barrett with Libby Gausden, 1961

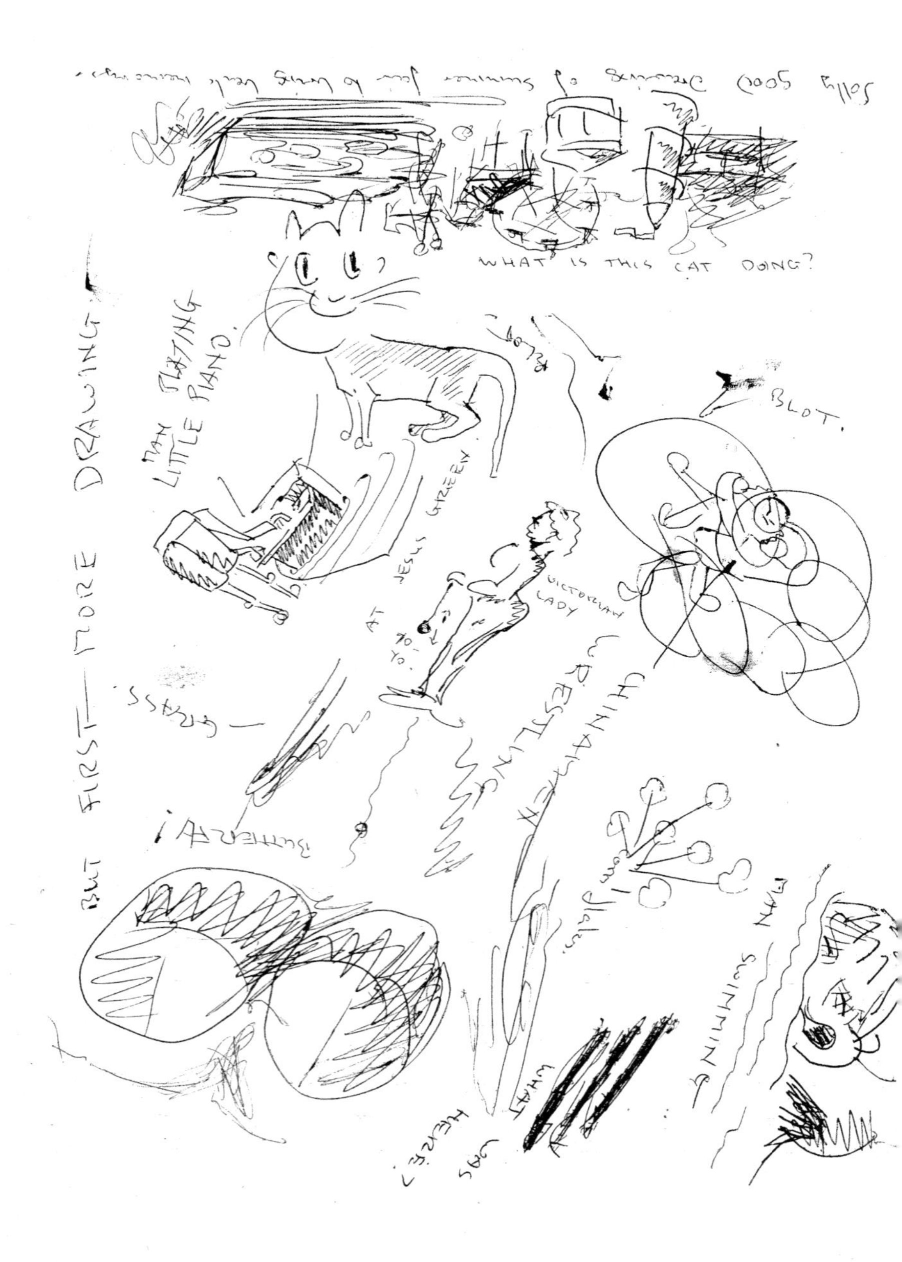
WHAT IS THIS CAT DOING?
BUT FIRST— MORE DRAWING:
MAN PLAYING LITTLE PIANO.
AT JESUS GREEN
VICTORIAN LADY
BLOT.
CHINAMEN WRESTLING
MAN SWIMMING
WHAT WAS HERE?

Above: Barrett has a Hamlet moment, 1964
Left: a page of sketches from one of his many letters to Libby Gausden

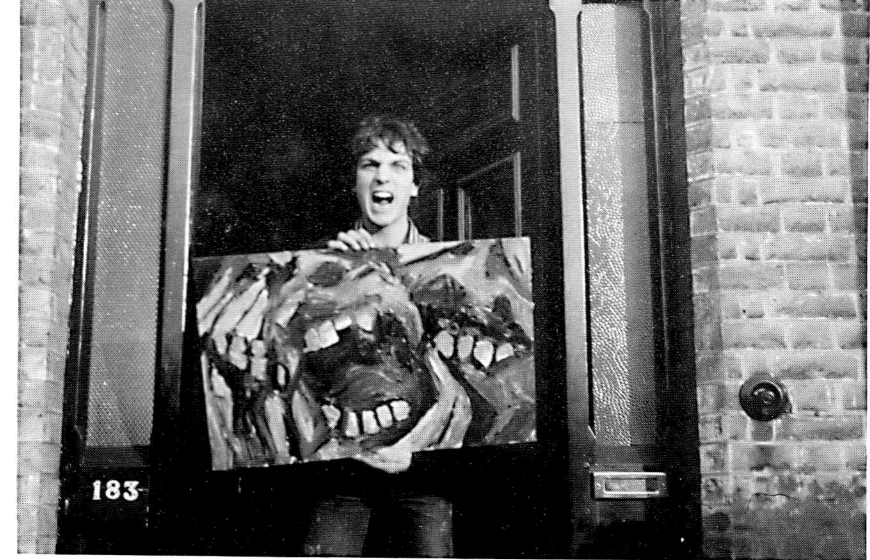
183

Right: Barrett and Gausden at Skegness Butlin's, 1963

Below right: the pair are joined by Roe for breakfast

Left: Barrett fronts the Hollerin' Blues, 1963

Below left: the Cambridge Tech student displays his work outside the family home in Hills Road, 1964

Above: Barrett with moustache and mirror-decorated Fender, 1966
Right: Lindsay Corner. *Overleaf*: psychedelia personified, 1967

Redferns Music Picture Library

Byrds and the sardonic Fugs – and he would make their styles his own, too. For Barrett was busy now, creating such vehicles as 'Interstellar Overdrive' for the 'psychedelic' jams which the four-man Floyd, through musical incompetence, made their speciality. They practised round at Cromwell Road, and acted as house-band for the Lesmoir-Gordons' happenings downstairs, where more primitive (but excellent) light-shows took place. But apart from that, they hardly saw each other.

A year or so later, Barrett would be living in Cromwell Road, and on the edge of breakdown. But if ever he was happy, it was now: sitting on Earlham Street's flat roof, smoking dope, and sometimes opium; playing guitars; popping down to the Pollo Bar for an ice-cream; talking about drugs and the meaning of life. He taught Freddie Venn, a girl who was passing through, how to make pancakes. Meanwhile, Lindsay weaned him off his bumfluff pencil moustache. An expert seamstress, over the next few months she would help him to develop his (and her) signature look of permed hair and eyeliner – kind of Dylan meets Jagger – with frilly shirts, fancy waistcoats and a straggling kerchief knotted round the neck; the boots were Gohills, the trousers tapered, not flared. In their glad rags, the gang would make acid-fuelled expeditions to see Guy the Gorilla (again) and *The Messiah* at the Albert Hall. And of course, that's the other thing: if ever there was time for Barrett to take LSD, it was now.

None of the survivors thinks the acid did him any harm then. Storm Thorgerson even has a theory that constant female attention did him more damage. Certainly, Lindsay Corner noticed a nasty streak in Barrett, when she found him holding court to other girls: 'He'd sit there, with his legs crossed, giving me this really evil eye.' For a couple of months, she would go to live with her younger Ely friend Gala Pinion, while he had a serious affair with the Cambridge exile Jenny Spires – and a less serious one with Kari-Ann Moller, now married to Mick Jagger's brother Chris.

The Floyd only had two gigs in the rest of the year. In November, they played at a riotous 21st birthday party in Cambridge for the January sisters, daughters of a rich property developer. (Also on the bill were Jokers Wild and the young Paul Simon, and they all jammed together at the end.) The next month, they were at the newly fashionable Goings-On club in Archer Street, London, where Peter Brown had started poetry-with-music evenings.

Not until '66 did they achieve cult status with the growing counter-culture in the capital, now headlined by *Time* magazine as 'Swinging London' – a phrase encompassing the myriad little scenes, with no respect for old social divisions, that had sprung up under the wings of the Beatles and the Stones.

Today, their names are inscribed in the pantheon of popular culture: Twiggy and the Shrimp, Peter Blake and David Hockney, Hung on You and Bailey's Youthquake. The swingers bought their textiles, art and books at the Indica Gallery, set up by Peter Asher, the pop-star brother of the actess Jane, who was dating Paul McCartney.* Their new stereos rattled to the scorching guitars of the Who, the Troggs and the Kinks. While the younger ones watched *Ready Steady Go!*, and queued behind the velvet rope at the Scotch of St James's, the more sophisticated were to be seen at the Ad-Lib club, the ICA – where the light-artist Mark Boyle was now staging events – and the Goings-On.

Inspired by such events, John Hopkins teamed up with the promoter Steve Stollman to produce their own

* Indeed McCartney donated specially printed wrapping-paper to the shop – where Lennon also first met Yoko Ono.

Sunday-afternoon happenings at the Marquee Club. Promising 'music, dancing, painting, sculpture', and urging punters to 'TRIP, bring furniture toy prop paper rug' and so on, these multimedia events were billed as 'The Spontaneous Underground'. Through Lesmoir-Gordon, the Floyd met Stollman, who tried out Barrett's band in early spring, and began to book them every few weeks. By April, such mods-turned-hippies as Malcolm McLaren (later the Sex Pistols' manager) and David Bowie (then known as Davey Jones) were Barrett's biggest fans. By May, Lesmoir-Gordon's friends Peter Jenner and Andrew King were on to him.

Since graduating, Jenner had become a lynchpin to the various sub-groups who would coalesce the next year to waste the 'official' Summer of Love. A lecturer at the LSE, his fingers were in all sorts of pies: a 'record production company', the nascent Notting Hill Carnival, the Free School (a nice idea, with no premises, that never actually taught anyone anything) and the upcoming freaks' paper, the *International Times* (*IT*). The richer King, who was leaving his job in airline PR, had known Jenner since childhood and was partner in some of these crimes. Both saw the commercial potential of the

Marquee scene, and King had his severance pay to spend.

If they were impressed by Barrett, they had to deal with Waters. He told the pair that the Floyd would probably break up, unless these prospective managers could put in some money. They agreed to talk after the summer holidays, when King offered to loan them enough to pay for their growing crew, new equipment and a £5 weekly wage. King and Jenner styled the six-way partnership Blackhill Enterprises, after a cottage that they owned in Wales. The deal was done by September – when the Floyd played an *IT* fund-raiser at the All Saints Hall, off Ladbroke Grove – and formally signed on 31 October. Waters, Wright and Mason had suspended or finished their studies by then, though Barrett was still nominally at art school.

Signing the contract, he may have felt that he had put Mammon before God. Religion had been all the rage among the Cambridge crowd that summer. A good two years before the Beatles, the Lesmoir-Gordons and friends had travelled to India and found themselves a guru. They became *satsangi*, or followers, of Maharaji Charan Singh Ji – 'the Master' – who preached love and transcendence in a strange form of Hinduism called Sant

Mat, which is based on the Gospel of Saint Matthew. Initiates did not have to wear robes or live in ashrams, but were forbidden meat, drinks and drugs.

To be honest, it's surprising that Barrett was at all interested, but he certainly bought the Master's book – and eagerly passed it on to Andrew Rawlinson. When the guru went on tour, Barrett attended his lectures at a London hotel. While many friends were initiated, however, Barrett was not. A very rare event among the *satsangi*, this rejection was either due to his youth or his drug intake. Twice he asked the Master and twice was refused without explanation. Again according to Thorgerson, these incidents also had a worse effect on him than all the stress and drugs.

By now, Barrett was already well on the way to stardom. He wrote 'Matilda Mother', that evocation of the moment between the bedtime-story ending and lights-out. And the Floyd supported the Soft Machine's experimental jazz-rock at *IT*'s launch party, a 2,000-strong happening in the disused Roundhouse theatre, featuring acid aplenty, Marianne Faithfull dressed as a nun in a pussy-pelmet, and Paul McCartney disguised as an Arab. There was a giant jelly and a Pop Art-painted Cadillac, a mini-cinema and a performance piece by Yoko Ono. 'All apparently very psychedelic,' sniffed the *Sunday Times* of the Floyd, thus encouraging hundreds of difficult teenagers to check out their new residency at the All Saints Hall.

Now once- or twice-weekly, the shows took time to take off. Juliet Wright remembers an occasion when there were so few punters that Barrett movingly recited Hamlet's 'To be or not to be' soliloquy on-stage. But soon ravers were crossing London for the lights and the weirdness, titillated by music-press adverts using Timothy Leary's phrase of 'Turn on, Tune in, Drop out'. With Barrett's nursery-rhyme freak-outs lasting 40 minutes each, the Floyd become known as Britain's first 'psychedelic' band – even though they did it by default. Apart from the drugs, the King's Road clothes and the 'free love', Barrett seemed blithely unaware of most developments in the wider hippie world to which he later became so important.

Gilmour dropped in on an All Saints gig, en route to France, where the remnants of Jokers Wild planned to try their luck under the name of Bullet; he thought the Floyd made 'a horrible din'. But for 15-year-old Emily Young, known as 'Far Out Em', the venue would have a special significance. A daughter of the Labour politician Lord Kennett, she was a student at the then-trendy Holland Park state school, where her best friend was Angelica Huston, daughter of the fashionable film director. The pair were fixtures on the London music scene, where they were presumed to be in their late teens. One night, after an All Saints gig, they went with the band to Jenner's house nearby, shared a joint and got rapping with Barrett; the next year, he wrote the acid-pop classic 'See Emily Play'. Starring the girl who 'tries but misunderstands' and 'always borrows somebody's dreams till tomorrow', it's a memorial to the starry-eyed teenybopper – though naturally Barrett told the press that the song came to him in a vision, after he woke up in a wood.

Soon the Floyd were landing college gigs outside the capital, and high-profile events within (a couple of Roundhouse billings, a slot in an Oxfam benefit at the Albert Hall). In January '67, after a try-out the month before, they began a residency at the famous UFO – 'Yoo-Fo' – club. These mini-Roundhouse raves, called 'Night Trippers', ran from 10pm to 4.30am fortnightly. Co-promoted by the Anglophile American Joe Boyd, they were held in the Blarney pub's basement on Tottenham Court Road – and the Pink Floyd went down a storm. For the rest of Barrett's tenure in the band, they were to be idolised by hip metropolitan audiences like UFO's – and bottled and spat upon in the discotheques of the less experimentally inclined provinces.

What a gruelling year that was, from beginning to end. Apart from playing a packed live schedule, the Floyd were in pursuit of a recording contract, rehearsing and making rough demos. Joe Boyd, who had production experience, took them into a studio in late January. Barrett had written 'Arnold Layne' by then, rewritten 'Let's Roll Another One' for wider consumption as 'Candy and a Currant Bun', and perfected the relentless riff of 'Interstellar Overdrive'. EMI – the same label as the Beatles! – signed them up on the basis of these demos, nominating 'Arnold' as the first single; and ahead of their time the Floyd made two promotional shorts with a director-friend. For 'Arnold', they messed around with a mannequin on a Sussex beach. For its future B-side, 'Scarecrow', they trooped around cornfields with one of their own. Barrett was delighted. 'We want to be pop stars,' he said, gladly grinning for cheesy publicity shots of the band high-kicking on the street. However, by the beginning of April, he was already railing in the music papers against record-company executives – 'the middlemen' – who were pressing him for more commercial material.

He was even less cheery by the end of the month. Six weeks before, 'Arnold Layne' had been released. This jolly tale of Mary Waters' washing-line raider was helped up the charts by a ban from Radio London, due to its lyrics about transvestism – and by some shady hyping – but Barrett had grown to hate playing note-perfect, three-minute renditions on stage. On 22 April it reached number 20, its highest position. On 29 April Barrett was still playing it, in UFO at dawn and on a TV show in Holland that evening. The band then drove back to London to headline at 3am in Britain's biggest happening ever, the '14 Hour Technicolor Dream' at the cavernous Alexandra Palace.

It was an extremely druggy affair. Jenner was certainly tripping that night, and Barrett is said to have been. John Lennon, Brian Jones and Jimi Hendrix were in the 10,000-strong audience. There were 40 bands, dancers in strobe shows, a helter-skelter, and a notice-board made of light bulbs which displayed messages like 'Vietnam Is A Sad Trip'. The Floyd came on as the sun's pink fingers touched the huge eastern window. Barry Miles, the Sixties chronicler, reported: 'Syd's eyes blazed as his notes soared up into the strengthening light, as the dawn was reflected in his famous mirror-disc Telecaster [or rather, Esquire].' The truth was less rosy. Barrett was tired, so terribly tired.

***

There's a horrible ring of truth to Sue Kingsford's contention that, in '67, Barrett would regularly visit her and Jock in Beaufort Street, to score from a heavy acid dealer in the basement called 'Captain Bob'. On the other hand, as Andrew Rawlinson says: 'Whether Syd was tripping himself or not, he could easily have "picked up" on other people who were. If you had taken a lot of acid in the past, you could find yourself tripping again just by observing someone else on acid.'

It certainly sounds more likely than the rumours that Barrett's camp-followers were lacing his breakfast tea with LSD. Jock says: 'Spiking was a heinous crime. You just wouldn't do it. There was a ritual to acid taking in those days – a peaceful scene, good sounds [or 'set and setting', as Leary called it].'

David Gilmour reckons: 'Syd didn't need encouraging. If drugs were going, he'd take them by the shovelful.' Gilmour tends to agree with something Waters once said – that 'Syd was being fed acid'. But Sue Kingsford giggles: 'We were all feeding it to each other.' She doesn't remember 'set and setting' being so important by then: 'It was a crazy time.' Despite her attachment to Jock, she had a one-night stand with Barrett. 'We were tripping,' she explains.

Ah, but what does she mean by tripping? Rawlinson again: 'Acid in those days was five times stronger than today's stuff. On a proper trip, you might take 250 micrograms. But a faction believed in taking 50mcg every day. [There was even a popular hippie-handbook on the subject.] On that, you could function – you might even appear normal – but you couldn't initiate much.'

Perhaps that was Barrett's way. But if he had actually taken a proper dose of acid at the Technicolor Dream, then it was a fairly rare event. He simply didn't have the time for anything stronger than dope – which he did smoke in copious quantities. And maybe for a few Mandrax, the hypnotic tranquillisers which, if one can ride the first wave of tiredness, induce a opiate-like buzz when swallowed with alcohol. In legend, 'Mandies make you randy.' About as dangerous as heroin, they may have appealed to Barrett because they were fashionable in the late Sixties – or because they stopped his mind from spinning.

He, Rover the cat and Corner had taken a room at Cromwell Road in the New Year, when the scene there was already closing down. The *satsangi* Lesmoir-Gordons had gone to the Egerton Court pad, and the ground floor was boarded up, pending demolition of the building. Duggie Fields, Jock and Sue were on their way out of the maisonette, and characters like the photographer Mick Rock, a Cambridge graduate, were moving in. But Barrett was so busy, he was hardly there. He only chucked his course at the end of January. Three weeks later, he was gigging three or four times a week, giving interviews to the press and television, stepping on the treadmill of stardom.

The band bought a dodgy old Rolls-Bentley with shot brakes – which Barrett was forbidden from driving – and that must have eased the travelling. Even so, he was spending most of his days off the road in EMI's huge studio complex, behind its little white house on Abbey Road. There, for the next five months, the band would record the Floyd's first album, *Piper at the Gates of Dawn* – not with Joe Boyd producing, as Barrett would have preferred, but with the rather straight Norman Smith. Foisted on the Floyd by EMI, Smith had cut his teeth as George Martin's sound engineer on the Beatles until 1965.*

It was an unlikely, but winning combination (though Pete Townshend always hated the LP's quaintness, when compared with the trippy live shows). Smith grumpily controlled Barrett's excesses as the rhyme-scheme does a sonnet – but to listen to him, you'd think he'd suffered the worst of Barrett's 1968 sessions with Peter Jenner, when our hero's mind was briefly muddled by barbiturates, smack and illness.

'I wonder how we managed to get anything together,' said Smith. 'Working with Syd was sheer hell and there

* While the Floyd were recording *Piper*, the Beatles were actually working on *Sergeant Pepper* in the studio next door. (Hence the Syd-on-*Pepper* myth.) The two bands met only once, when Lennon was standoffish and McCartney chummy.

are no pleasant memories. I don't think I left a single Floyd session without a splitting headache. Syd never seemed to have any enthusiasm for anything. He'd be singing a song and I'd call him into the control room to give him a few instructions. Then he'd go back out and not even sing the first part the same, let alone the bit I'd been talking about. Sometimes he even changed the words – he had no discipline. Trying to talk to him was like trying to talk to a brick wall because his face was so expressionless. His lyrics were simple and childlike and he was like a child in many ways – up one minute and down the next. I often wondered what the hell he was doing in the music business... Syd seemed to get more of a kick out of meeting [the Beatles] than he did out of being in the Floyd.'

Picasso's framer probably didn't get the point either, but there you go. To be fair to Smith, Lindsay Corner thought Barrett had been acting more and more oddly for months. She'd get home from her boutique or modelling jobs, 'And he just wasn't there. It was distressing. He didn't have normal conversations. I thought I could rescue him. I'd talk to him for hours on end, even convince him to see a professional. Then I'd realise I hadn't got through at all.' And to be fair to Barrett, he hadn't reckoned on the hassle of making product for EMI.

Jenner speaks admiringly of Barrett's unique technique on the mixing desks: 'He would throw the levers on the board up and down, apparently at random, making pretty patterns with his hands... He wouldn't do anything unless he was doing it in an artistic way.' Barrett wanted to be an aural Jackson Pollock – creating in the moment, not churning out note-perfect repeat performances. But the avant-garde could be as hostile as the proletariat: on 8 April, when the Floyd played their new single 'Arnold' at the Roundhouse's 'All Night Light Continuum', Barrett had to endure a support group – the proto-punk Flies, dressed in war-paint and hula-skirts – shouting 'Sell-out!' at him from the wings.

The band weren't too worried by his behaviour yet – Syd was Syd. And if, by the end of May, people who hadn't seen Barrett for a while thought he had changed, his month had started well. On 12 May, the band played the highfalutin 'Games for May' concert at one of the capital's classiest classical venues, the Queen Elizabeth Hall. Barrett wrote an early version of 'See Emily Play' for the event, which was essentially a normal concert book-ended by some pretentious bits. The Floyd introduced a rudimentary quad sound system, played taped noises from nature, and had a liquid-red light-show. Mason was amplified sawing a log. Waters threw potatoes at a gong. The roadies pumped out thousands of soap bubbles, and one of them, dressed as an admiral, threw daffodils into the stalls.

The mess earned the Floyd a ban from the hall and a favourable review from the *Financial Times*. Barrett said: 'In the future, groups are going to have to offer much more than just a pop show. They'll have to offer a well-presented theatre show' (which was prophetic, when one thinks of today's stadium-rock). Then Barrett and Waters appeared in one of those classic Sixties set-pieces on BBC Television, where the two spokesmen for alternative culture were quizzed by the Teutonic Hans Keller, a respected classical-music critic.

Keller's first question to Barrett was: 'If one gets immune to this kind of sound, one may find it difficult to appreciate softer types of sound? Syd? Yes? No?'

'I don't think that's so.'

'No?'

'I mean... everybody listens, we don't need it very loud

to be able to hear it, and some of it is very quiet in fact.'

'Right.'

'I – personally – I like quiet music just as much as loud music. We play in large halls and things, where obviously volume is necessary, and when people dance they like volume. You know, it comes on its own, but...'

'Well, that's very interesting, you see. "When people dance." You did start, if I'm not mistaken, as a group which accompanied dancing?'

Keller then asked if Barrett thought the concert-hall setting had been successful?

'Yes, I think so. With the – with us – when we play, I think the way the act's developed in the last six months has been influenced rather a lot by the fact that we've played in ballrooms necessarily.'

So there was no 'shock treatment' involved, asked Keller? 'No, certainly not! Some people think that we deliberately try to... shock the audience and... keep them quiet, sort of thing. But this isn't so.'

Keller finished by turning to his own audience: 'Well, there it is. I think you can pass your verdict as well as I can. My verdict is that it is a little bit of regression to childhood. But after all, why not?'

Barrett could be just as patronising himself. Judging that week's new chart releases for *Melody Maker*, he remarked of David Bowie's first single: 'It's a joke number... If you play it a second time, it might be even more of a joke... but I don't think my toes were tapping at all.' Then, in the middle of all this press, in the middle of recording the album and constantly touring, EMI wanted another single. Jenner decided on 'Emily' and – to recapture the twang of their first outing – he made a 21 May booking for the same independent studio that Boyd had used with 'Arnold'. King, borrowing the family flat in Richmond, installed Wright, Barrett and their partners into its two rooms. Rover was left with the freaks still in Cromwell Road; at a subsequent date, he may or may not have been fed LSD.

On 2 June, the Floyd played Boyd's UFO after a two-month absence. Though the other band members were friendly, Boyd says, Barrett 'just looked at me. I looked right in his eye and there was no twinkle, no glint... you know, nobody home.' Perhaps Barrett was embarrassed about the way Boyd had been dropped for Norman Smith, when the band had just used the same studio as Boyd? David Gilmour thinks not. Visiting London from

France, he dropped in on the recording of 'Emily': 'Syd didn't seem to recognise me and he just stared back,' says Gilmour. 'He was a different person from the one I'd last seen in October.' Was he on drugs, though? 'I'd done plenty of acid and dope – often with Syd, too – and that was different from how he had become.'*

Things got worse as the weeks passed. 'Emily' was released on 16 June, and on 6 July, the Floyd did their first *Top of the Pops*. Although Barrett had by now had one or two run-ins with broadcasters, his attitude to *TOTP* was distinctly puzzling. For the first show, he was enthusiastic, and wore his stage clothes: red shirt, red slippers and tapering black trousers. The second time, he forgot the appointment: Jenner had to race round to his flat to drag him out, and he appeared in his day clothes. The third time – on 27 July, when 'Emily' reached number six, its highest position – he turned up in his stage attire then changed into rags to perform. 'He was flouncing,' remembers Waters. 'He announced he wasn't going to do *Top of the Pops* any more: John Lennon didn't have to do it, so why should he! I thought, "What's getting into

* Gilmour revised this opinion a few weeks later. 'Now I'm leaning towards a "lost weekend" theory,' he says.

him?" I was half-impressed by how starrily he was behaving, and half of me thought, "How weird." '

Touring the provinces that month, like the rest of the band, Barrett resented the beery mob baying for 'Arnold' and 'Emily'. The Floyd even wrote a white-noise number called 'Reaction in G' to express their feelings. But Barrett's inner reaction was harder to fathom. With his echo-machines on full tilt, he might detune his Fender until its strings were flapping, and hit one note all night. He might stand with his arms by his side, the guitar hanging from his neck, staring straight ahead, while the others performed as a three-piece. He might decline to sing, forcing them to cover for him.

The author of the Barrett biography *Lost in the Woods* is reminded of Nijinsky's final performance, when the mad dancer sat, motionless and silent, for half an hour, eyes blazing at his audience. Juliet Wright says: 'It's funny what you get used to. Often we thought he was just being non-conformist in the conformist situation of a band.' Perhaps, obliged to be there in body if not in spirit, Barrett was making a statement. Perhaps he was pushing his experimental notions of 'music-of-the-moment' to new boundaries (and damn the others and the consequences). Whatever else, he was now seriously mentally ill. And almost certainly he suspected it himself.

Waters definitely did. He poured out his woes to his mother – 'They were feeding him LSD in that flat' – and she passed on his concerns to Win. Win's second son Alan was dispatched to visit his brother in London, where Barrett convinced him that there was nothing wrong. Wynne-Wilson remembers that Barrett had 'a devastating smile which he would sometimes use to pretend he was okay'. It must have worked on Alan: Roger was Roger, he said – and, as Waters admits, 'Syd couldn't have controlled himself. He couldn't fool someone who didn't want to be fooled.'

Roe, now a student nurse in London, had a more unsettling encounter. When 'Arnold' came out, she had sent Barrett a congratulatory letter from her lodgings in Terrapin Road (a name that he would later use in one of his best solo songs). But after the release of 'Emily', when they met during the holidays at Hills Road, 'he'd changed so much that I just couldn't reach him. The brother I knew had disappeared.' Roe, who has always blamed the drugs for his breakdown, continued: 'After that meeting, I just couldn't enjoy the music any more.'

Jenner and King should have called a halt after Barrett pulled out of a radio recording on 28 July, causing it to be cancelled; or the next night, after the 'International Love-In' at the Alexandra Palace. This event turned out to be Britain's mini-Altamont, where, according to *Melody Maker*, 'flower power and music were ground into the litter-laden floor'. The bouncers were violent, the crowds of weekend hippies were terrified by gangs of hostile locals, and a lad was stabbed in the lashing rain that swept the carpark. A catatonic Barrett had to be pulled on-stage, where he was unable to stand, and the band legged it with their fee after playing four numbers.

In the end, a similar débâcle in Devon, two days later, forced Jenner and King to act. Though *Piper* was released on 4 August, Blackhill cancelled the next three weeks' gigs, and arranged a holiday at the end of the month for Barrett and Corner on the Balearic island of Formentera. Sam Hutt and Rick Wright would be chaperones, accompanied by their partners and Hutt's baby son. Waters and his wife would be a ferry-ride away in Ibiza. When *Melody Maker* learned of this, their front-page splash read: 'PINK FLOYD FLAKE OUT'.

It is a measure of Barrett's music that, within months

of turning professional, his band was a top news story. He had achieved something remarkable. Those who saw the Floyd live in London at the time speak as though they were up the scaffolding with Michelangelo, or peering over Shelley's shoulder. (David Gilmour admits that 'they must have improved dramatically' in the months since he had last seen them.) Barrett brought all the stagecraft that he'd learned at school to his performances. While molten light-shapes slid over him, he made the big, bold movements of an officiating high priest. His group would create the aural equivalent of an acid trip, slowly bringing the audience up and down, while Barrett pierced the darkness with his crisply enunciated word-pictures of stoical scarecrows and space odysseys.

On vinyl, the experience was like a flashback. 'Arnold', 'Emily' and such *Piper* songs as 'Interstellar Overdrive' and 'Astronomy Domine' are benchmarks in the history of electric music – forever of their period and forever fresh – giving a unique, hallucinatory take on English sensibilities and eccentricities. Sometimes Barrett can verge on the twee – 'A gnome called Grimble-Gromble' springs to mind* – but usually the lyrics

* Bowie's homage to this was the embarrassing 'Laughing Gnome'.

are childish in the best sense: wide-eyed, dreamlike, sometimes nightmarish. With a few words, Barrett can tell a story. ('Arnold Layne had a strange hobby./ Collecting clothes./ Moonshine, washing line./ They suit him fine.') In 'Matilda Mother', with its 'doll's house darkness old perfume', he shows signs of the poet he would become. He was already an incredibly sophisticated musician: interweaving delicate sound-effects with thudding bass and drums, he creates an effect that is wholly original; that captures the spirit of the age as much as *Sergeant Pepper* – but more coolly, with wit and style.

Music critics, rightly, raved over the album, which reached number six in the charts. But the unfortunate consequence was that EMI demanded *another* single, sharpish. Though Waters' writing talent was beginning to emerge, for the moment the Floyd had to rely on Barrett – and he wasn't up to being commercial. Kari-Ann Jagger's abiding impression of him at the time is of being 'immensely frustrated'.

His state of mind can be guessed at from his offering for 7 August: 'Scream Thy Last Scream, Old Woman in a Casket' is an ear-splitting mess whose title-line is its most redeeming feature. EMI rightly turned it down, and told Jenner and King that they expected something better once Barrett had returned from his break.

For the fortnight in Formentera, Barrett was 'sweet', remembers Juliet Wright. Lindsay Corner recalls him 'wandering off a lot – and you'd find him practising on Sam's sitar under a far-off fig-tree'. Of course, he was horribly sunburned. And when there was a lightning storm, Juliet says that he was 'literally climbing up the walls – he disappeared and slept in a graveyard for three days'. Oh, and once, he spilt hot coffee over Sam Hutt's son, 'which made him very low – he was devastated all day'. But the holiday was otherwise uneventful.

Back in London, the frontman was shoved back into harness, criss-crossing the British Isles and Scandinavia through September and October. Hiding from EMI in the De Lane Lea Studios, in Kingsway, London, he spent more and more fruitless studio time in trying to find a single. One attempt was 'Vegetable Man'. Often cited as incontrovertible proof of his lunacy, the song was inspired by an interview Barrett gave in the studio to a reporter from *Go!* magazine.

Barrett explained that what he was searching for

was spontaneity and 'thinking less', to which the journalist replied: 'You might as well be a vegetable.' 'Yeah,' grinned Barrett. Looking at what he was wearing, he later wrote: 'In yellow shoes/I get the blues,/So I walk the street with my plastic feet,/With blue velvet trousers. Make me feel pink./There's a kind of stink about blue velvet trousers.'

It continues in the same vein – 'In my paisley shirt/I look a jerk/... Vegetable Man, where are you?' – and finishes with psychotic shouting: 'And all the luck,/ It's what I got,/It's what I wear,/It's what you see,/It must be me/... I've been looking all over the place/For a place for me/But it ain't anywhere./It just ain't anywhere.'

This wasn't even progressive material, let alone commercial. Waters found it plain disturbing. The band felt that, if Barrett's singles muse had deserted him, then his erratic behaviour was hard to bear. But, despite this uncomfortable atmosphere, they managed to lay down a couple of numbers by Waters and Wright for the next album, *Saucerful of Secrets*. And Barrett came up with a track called 'Jugband Blues'.

'It's awfully considerate of you to think of me here,' he sneers at his bandmates in the first verse. 'And I'm most obliged to you for making it clear/That I'm not here.' There follows perhaps an abstruse reference to *TOTP*: 'And I'm grateful that you threw away my old shoes/And brought me here instead dressed in red.' The verse ends with a reminder that – however much his colleagues might complain about his lack of productivity – 'I'm wondering who could be writing this song?'

Or maybe he actually was wondering. With hindsight, the track has been recognised as a seminal Barrett piece. But at the time, with a US mini-tour looming – and EMI demanding that, before departing, the Floyd come up with the goods for the Christmas domestic market – what the boys really needed was a *single*.

***

A bungle saved their bacon. Although they were meant to have been playing the West Coast in the last week of October, their work visas didn't come through in time, and several dates had to be dropped from the tour. In the intervening days, Barrett wrote 'Apples and Oranges', a musical sketch of Lindsay Corner shopping in Richmond. The critics were divided over this song, released in mid-November; the public were united in ignoring it; but the band were relieved to have had it accepted by EMI. According to Waters, 'By now, Syd was way out there. He thought he was a homosexual, and he'd get into the car in drag.' (It would be some years until Bowie would make such cross-dressing acceptable.) Jenner stayed in London, to sort out the single's release. The Floyd flew to California with King – and some apprehension.

Had they seen the future, they would have panicked. They were not prepared for the American way. They had expected the San Francisco scene to be similar to Britain's. Instead, they found themselves in humungous venues like the Winterland, supporting such blues bands as Big Brother and the Holding Company (led by Janis Joplin). The three nights they played with Joplin, they borrowed her lighting because their own seemed so weedy. The crowd weren't into feedback or English whimsy – acid-inspired or not. Barrett was off the map, and when he did play, it was to a different tune.

At the beginning of the week, his hair had been badly permed at Vidal Sassoon, and he was distraught at the effect. The greased-up 'punk' style, with which he'd been experimenting, would be better. Waters remembers that, in the dressing-room at the Cheetah Club in Santa Monica, Barrett suddenly called for a tin of Brylcreem and tipped the whole lot on his head. Producing a bottle of Mandrax, he crushed them into the mess before taking the stage. David Gilmour says he 'still can't believe that Syd would waste good Mandies'. But a lighting-man called John Marsh, who was also there, confirms the story. As the gunk melted, it slipped down his face until Barrett resembled 'a gutted candle'. Girls in the front row, seeing his lips and nostrils bubbling with Brylcreem, screamed. He looked like he was decomposing on-stage.

Faced with this farce, some of the band and crew abandoned themselves to drink, drugs, groupies and the sights. When they arrived in Los Angeles, Barrett had forgotten his guitar, which caused much cost and fuss. 'It's great to be in Las Vegas,' he said to a record-company man in Hollywood. He fell into a swimming-pool and left his wet clothes behind. Though she may be confusing another incident, Libby Gausden also claims that he bought an old Cadillac and gave it away to a passer-by.

The Floyd survived the tour by the skin of their teeth. On TV's *Pat Boone Show*, where they did 'Apples and

Oranges', Barrett was happy to mime in rehearsals – but live he ignored the call to 'Action' four or five times, leaving Waters to fill in. Asked what he liked in the after-show chat, Barrett replied... after a dreadful pause... 'America!', which made the audience whoop. On *American Bandstand* and the *Perry Como Show*, he did not move his lips, to speak or mime.

Finishing their commitments on the West Coast, the band played one night at the Cheetah in New York, and came home. During the flight, Waters demanded that King solve 'the Syd problem', and the band began thinking of how to replace or augment him. The next day, they were in Holland, handing the mute Barrett notes in the hope that he would talk to them. The day after, they were bus-bound on a British package tour with Hendrix, the Move, Amen Corner, the Nice and others, playing two 17-minute sets a night for three weeks, with three days off in the middle.

Though he had worked harder, the schedule was far too much for Barrett. When he went on-stage, he was unable to function. Sometimes he failed to show up and the Nice's Dave O'List stood in for him. Once, Jenner had to stop him escaping by train. Asked by *Melody*

Maker about the failure of 'Apples and Oranges', Barrett said: 'I couldn't care less.'

Back in London, however, he was soon checking the scene at such up-and-coming venues as the Speakeasy and the Middle Earth club. And, surprisingly, the Lesmoir-Gordons claim that Barrett took an acid trip with them at Blackhill Cottage at the end of November. Jenny later described him as 'a bit of a nuisance', with Nigel adding 'a court jester' – which seems a bit mean, when Lesmoir-Gordon went on to profit from the sale of *Syd's* [so-called] *First* [mushroom] *Trip*. Anyway, there was certainly no LSD around at Richmond – even if Rick Wright was 'freaking out', as Juliet describes it, 'You know: "Should I leave, should I go with Syd, what should I do?"' Lindsay Corner says she was 'really struggling hard to keep Syd sane'. Both recall his stare becoming even more frightening – but the band was touring so much, he was hardly home.

Barrett could – and did – play occasional blinders throughout the autumn of '67, but these instances were as unpredictable as spring showers, and the band's hopes that he might 'return' dimmed. The Floyd stumbled through to Christmas, while the three well ones hatched

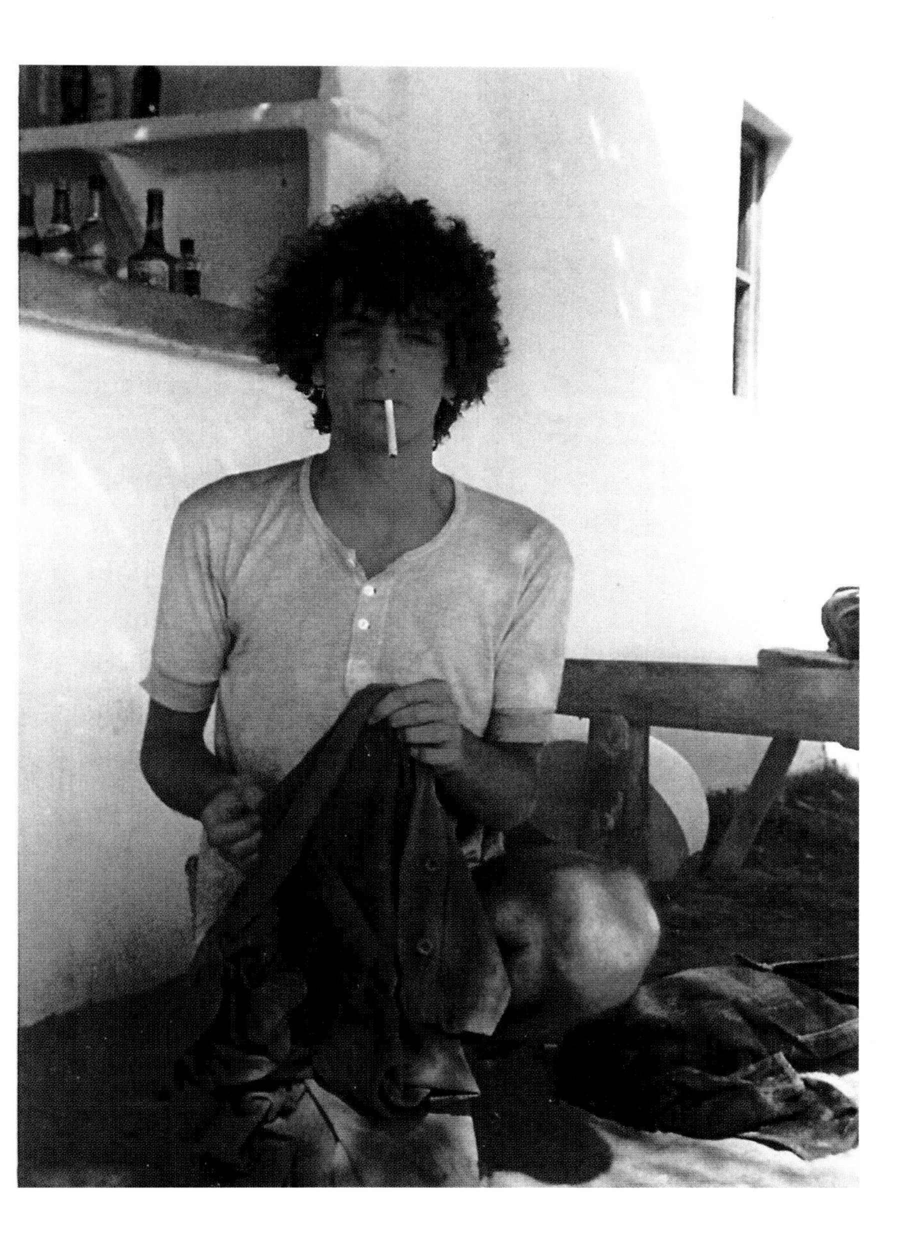

Above and overleaf: on holiday in Formentera, 1967

Previous page: left to right, Roger Waters, Sam Hutt (aka Hank Wangford) and Barrett meet up on Formentera, 1967

Above and left: Barrett and Lindsay Corner in Andrew King's Richmond flat, which they shared with Rick Wright and Juliet Gale, 1967

Above: the five-man Pink Floyd with Barrett (second left) and David Gilmour (centre), 1968

a plan (or subconsciously dusted it off?): they would ask David Gilmour to join the group to cover lead guitar and vocals, while their sick colleague could do what he wanted, so long as he stood on-stage.

Barrett couldn't care, more or less, and Gilmour – back from France, broke, bandless and driving a van at the Quorum boutique, for whom Lindsay Corner also modelled – was known to be not only a terrific guitarist but also a wonderful mimic of musical parts. Nick Mason had already sounded him out when they ran into each other at a gig in Soho. On 3 January 1968, Gilmour was offered, and accepted, a try-out. The band had a week booked in a north London rehearsal hall before going back on the road.

The most famous Barrett incident that week took place when he arrived at the hall and announced that he had written a new song called 'Have You Got It Yet?'. He would sing the question, and Waters should answer 'No'. Imagine him playing a one-two rhythm on a guitar: 'Have you *got-it* yet?' [One-*two*, one-*two*, 'No'.] 'Have you *got-it* yet?' [One-*two*, one-*two*, 'No'.] Then higher: 'Have you *got-it* yet?'. Then lower: 'Have you *got-it* yet?' Waters picks up the tune, but Barrett now changes it, going lower, higher, anything but the same. This goes on five or six times, but still Barrett keeps changing. 'No, no no!' screams Waters. 'It wasn't until later that I realised what he was doing,' he now says. Barrett was asking him not to 'get' a song which (and a person who) was impossible to get. An absurdist work of performance art.

Four gigs followed in the next fortnight, with Barrett contributing little. He looks happy enough in a cine-clip from the time, joining in with the lads for an arms-over-the-shoulders tap-dance in a dressing-room. 'But in reality,' says Gilmour, 'he was rather pathetic.' On the day of the fifth gig – at Southampton on 26 January – the others were driving south from a business meeting in central London, towards Richmond. As they crossed the junction of Holland Park Avenue and Ladbroke Grove, one of them – no one remembers who – asked, 'Shall we pick up Syd?' 'Fuck it,' said the others. 'Let's not bother.' Barrett, who probably didn't notice that night, would never again work with the band that he had crafted in his image. And they never quite put him out of their minds.

Not that their minds were made up. Though the Floyd would go on to huge fame and fortune, at the time they believed they probably had a few months left of milking psychedelia before ignominious disbandment. Barrett, as Waters says, was the 'goose that had laid the golden egg'. Now their frontman had become such a liability on tour, they would rather appear without their main attraction than risk his involvement.

If, in retrospect, this has come to be seen as one of the most momentous fall-outs in the history of rock, at the time none of the participants realised its significance – perhaps because the bust-up was dragged out over several weeks. Wright began telling his flatmate that he was popping out for a packet of fags – then disappearing for days on tour.

However, Barrett still had the band's schedule. Waters remembers him turning up with his guitar at 'an Imperial College gig, I think, and he had to be very firmly told that he wasn't coming on stage with us'. At the Middle Earth, wearing all his Chelsea threads, he positioned himself in front of the low stage and stared at Gilmour throughout his performance. The 'Fred plan' had been for Gilmour to join Barrett's band, not supplant him in it. Now he had to watch his Tech friend playing *his* licks. Undoubtedly, he felt hurt by his treatment – and still does when forced to think about it.

An early plan was that Barrett could be like Brian Wilson from the Beach Boys, the group's genius and writer, who at the time no longer played live. Hopefully, he'd write a single for them to tour (and without which, they thought, they were doomed). It was put to Jenner and King, who relayed it to Barrett, who seemed pleased with the arrangement. However, Jenner and King may have already screwed up. In early January, they had booked Barrett and some other musicians into the Sound Techniques studio, the scene of his earliest triumph; they emerged without concrete results, and may thus have confused him.

A couple of weeks later, at a meeting with Jenner, King and Barrett, Waters was amazed to discover that – far from accepting his Wilson role – 'Syd was now talking about rejoining the band, along with a saxophonist and some other female' (an idea ahead of its time, when one thinks of the haunting arrangements on *Dark Side of the Moon*). The four sane Floyds gave up. Blackhill Enterprises was dissolved on 2 March, and the group went under new management. On 6 April Barrett officially left, retaining as his managers Jenner and King. In hindsight, it's amazing that these two, despite their client's behaviour, had more faith in his future than that of Pink Floyd.* At the time, their hope may have seemed less futile.

However, it was misplaced. They were unable to help him. No one could – so there's no need to ask, 'Why didn't they?' Yet those closest to Barrett do feel the need to explain. 'We thought we could carry him through it.' 'We were young, inexperienced, perhaps we were selfish.' 'We couldn't force him into therapy.' 'We thought we could sort it out between us.' 'It was uncool to intervene.' 'We thought he had to work his way through it like R D Laing said.' 'We thought he was doing it on purpose.' 'We were too busy.' 'He was operating on a different level, man.' (An opinion which can sometimes make Gilmour quite cross.)

Barrett's real friends tried even harder to help him in the years to come. But for now, as Juliet Wright says, 'They had actually given him an awful lot of chances.' The Richmond flat had not served Blackhill's purposes, and the scene there was uncomfortable, so King called the arrangement to a halt. Barrett and Lindsay Corner

* The Barrett-less Floyd kept their contract with EMI, and Barrett was given a new contract with the same company.

took a room in Egerton Court, joining Thorgerson, Po and David Gale. Then he hit rock bottom.

***

Where does one begin? Though the money from *Piper* came rolling in, Barrett's work went completely to pot. Jenner took him into the Abbey Road studios several times between May and July 1968, bringing various musicians and musical friends to help out, but achieved next to nothing: a few messy takes of songs which would later surface on the solo albums; and two jams called 'Rhamadan' and 'Lanky'.

Barrett was all over the place – forgetting to bring his guitar to sessions, breaking equipment to EMI's displeasure – and sometimes, he couldn't even hold his plectrum. God knows what the Blackhill boys thought they might achieve with him. He was in a state, and had little new material. Jenner had the experience neither as a person nor as a producer to coax anything out of him. By August, he and King were having less and less to do with Barrett – which could equally be said of the other lodgers in Egerton Court.

According to Po, 'Syd could still be very funny and very lucid, but he could also be uncommunicative. Staring. Heavy, you know.' The flat sounds a desperately unhappy place. 'We were all dealing with our own acid issues from the excesses of the year before,' Po continues, 'and when you're feeling that fragile, maybe you don't want to know about someone who – you know – there but for the grace of God...'

David Gale points out that there was no such thing as therapy for substance abuse in those days; no designer drugs for the mentally ill. Po adds that another Egertonian, a Cambridge lad nicknamed Ponji, was actually taking LSD with his psychiatrist to see his own bad experiences through to their conclusion. (He later committed suicide.) None the less, they did their best to help.

In the spring of '68, Roger Waters had talked to the hip psychiatrist RD Laing ('He was always a starfucker, so he knew of Syd'). He had even driven Barrett to an appointment: 'Syd wouldn't get out. What can you do?' In the intervening months, however, Barrett became less hostile to the idea of treatment. Now Gale placed a call to Laing, and Po booked a cab. But with the taxi-meter ticking outside, Barrett refused to leave the flat.* And he was causing havoc there. Po remembers him once hammering from inside the red-painted lavatory, 'Get me out! Get me out!' (Perhaps this was the occasion of Jonathan Meades' visit.) Though Po explained through the door that he would have to release the catch, 'It took Syd about an hour to work it out. When he emerged, he was sweating and trembling, like he'd had a fit.' Or indeed, an acid flashback.

Barrett took his frustrations out on Lindsay – beating her up, squeezing her between the bedroom door and its jamb until she screamed, burning her with cigarettes. 'Syd, we really don't think you should do that,' said his friends. 'What's it to you?' he replied. 'D'you wanna fight?' After he smashed the guitar over Lindsay, Po and Storm moved out. When Barrett burned all her clothes, Lindsay finally asked for help.

'We bundled her in a blanket into June Child's Mini,' remembers Juliet Wright. Then she and the Blackhill secretary smuggled her up to Storm's new place in

* Speaking to Gilmour some years later, Laing denied that he had ever heard of Barrett. The alcoholic Laing may have forgotten, of course. But, given the psychiatrist's posthumous reputation, it may be for the best that Barrett never met him.

Hampstead. But Barrett soon knew where Lindsay lived. He took to standing outside the house, ringing the bell, stalking her. Perhaps as revenge, he hit on her Ely side-kick Gala Pinion. Working as a waitress at the Chelsea Drugstore, Gala had followed Po to London, bringing with her Sasha, her West Highland Terrier. ('I was an impressionable 18-year-old with a rock star wanting to be my boyfriend,' she now says. 'I was thrilled.') He also sniffed around Iggy – a striking half-Eskimo who had previously gone out with Anthony Stern – and another girl working at Quorum called 'Silly' Gilly Staples.

By the autumn of '68, he was homeless. Periodically, he returned to Cambridge, where Win fretted, urged him to see a doctor, but perhaps blindly hoped for the best. In London, he crashed on friends' floors – and began the midnight ramblings which would continue for the next two years. Once, he had to run from the police after hanging out until dawn with the dopers at Holland Park youth hostel, and appeared at June Child's flat in Shepherd's Bush, covered in mud: 'I was still June, and "Office" had always made things right – it meant money, meant wages, meant security to him.' Often, barefoot, he headed south of the river to Battersea, whose inhabitants included Anthony Stern, Jenny Spires, and two speed freaks called Greta and Rusty. His welcome at Stern's became lukewarm, however, when he added heroin to his stash of hash and Mandrax: 'Syd would disappear to the loo every 40 minutes in a state of agitation and come back curiously calm.'

In fact, Barrett was getting better. It may seem crazy to say so – particularly considering the events that unfolded – but from now on he was recovering his sanity. The task took decades, and ultimately required him to withdraw from the world, but despite peaks and troughs, he began bumping up the seabed to the shore. He started in the New Year of 1969 by taking a three-bedroomed mansion flat in Earls Court Square with Duggie Fields and another friend who was soon replaced by Gala. Meanwhile, David Gilmour – who, as one of Pink Floyd, had enjoyed unexpected success with *Saucerful of Secrets* – rented a place in Old Brompton Road. Despite the troubled history and frightening present, he and Barrett had maintained a kind of friendship. They could see into each others' kitchens.

What dramas were to ensue. While keeping Gala as his serious girlfriend and Gilly Staples as a girlfriend,

Barrett began an affair with Iggy the Eskimo. This bizarre creature, surely the only half-Inuit among the Beautiful People, could look equally astonishing when out – knickerless, in her gold Forties gown with its train tied to her wrist – or wearing nothing at all, as she preferred indoors. (If she had a period, she wore a blood-stained nappy, made out of towels.) On top of these affairs, says Fields, Barrett had to cope with 'dozens of groupies, literally throwing themselves at him'.

The two men retreated behind locked doors – Fields to concentrate on his painting, Barrett to stop his flat-mate seeing the pictures that he claimed to be painting but wasn't. Says Fields: 'Syd spent most of his time in bed,' staring at the three sash windows and the intricate cornice. 'Lying on his mattress on the floor, you see, he had endless potential. A decision would have limited his options.' But that's not quite true. Barrett did start and abandon a couple of collages and mobiles. More importantly, in his head – and sometimes in feverish spurts of writing – he was working out some of the classic rock songs of all time; if you like what *Melody Maker* later called 'the mayhem and madness of the Barrett mind unleashed'.

By the end of March, various musicians had agreed to back him in the studio, including the Soft Machine. At the beginning of April, he rang his contemporary Malcolm Jones, the head of EMI's new 'alternative' Harvest label, and asked if he could record at Abbey Road. Luckily, Jones was a fan. He visited Earls Court to hear the tapes of the Jenner sessions, as well as some work in progress: 'Clowns and Jugglers' (renamed 'Octopus'), 'Terrapin', the jolly 'Love You' and two early songs, 'Golden Hair' and 'Here I Go'. Though Barrett's style had changed – these were mainly acoustic tracks, with his voice lower, flatter, stranger – Jones was 'elated'. The recordings began on 10 April 1969, with Jones as producer, because Barrett couldn't be bothered to name anyone else. None the less, three weeks later, he had laid down enough unmixed material for half an album.

Because of his erratic time signatures and key changes, because of his reluctance to repeat himself, take after take – because of his illness, his drug intake, his inability to communicate – these sessions have an undeservedly black reputation. Much has been made, for example, of a morning wasted when Barrett tried to dub some dud motorbike sounds on to 'Rhamadan', then lost interest. The recording techniques chosen – with musicians trying to follow Barrett's voice and guitar on a separate track, or vice versa, or with the band just busking behind him – have been produced as evidence of his unmanageability. Likewise, the number of takes. Well, some authorial revisionism is now necessary.

The number of takes should not detain us. According to Gilmour, 'Ten tries at a song is not a great score but it's not appalling.' On the other hand, you can't ignore that, when the Softs' Robert Wyatt asked Barrett what key he was in, he just said, 'Yeah!'; and when Wyatt pointed out that one song changed from two-and-a-half beats a bar to five, he replied: 'Oh really?' But Barrett's opinion of one passage – 'Perhaps we could make the middle darker and maybe the end a bit more middle-afternoonish [because] at the moment, it's too windy and icy' – sounds like synaesthesia in action.

And, in retrospect, Wyatt admits that Barrett was no trouble at all: 'I was brought up, musically, in the Fifties. If you want eccentricity, and that kind of non-verbal world, and those kind of weird signals that you have to pick up, you can't beat jazz musicians... The final recording was like the sketch of a painting never completed. Dead punk, when you come to think of it.'

David Gilmour has also mellowed over the *Madcap* sessions (in which he and Roger Waters later became involved). He once described them as 'hell'. Now he chuckles and calls them 'difficult – but inspired. On "Octopus", Syd suddenly chucks in a line from nowhere: "Little minute gong *coughs* and *clears* his throat." It has nothing, musically, to do with the song, but it works perfectly. The only other person who could break the timing rules like that – ignoring the number of beats to a bar in favour of the lyric – was John Lennon.' On a stylistic note, one might admire the musical mimicking of a creature coming up for air in 'Terrapin': 'You know the sunlight's *good* for us.'

The real trouble was that Barrett simply couldn't work fast enough – and, since he ran out of recording time, the mixes necessarily reflect his slapdash approach. However, for reasons to which we will return, some glitches drawing attention to Barrett's still-piteous state were left in – when they could have been erased – and these only served to fuel his legend.

Who, for example, can forget the disturbing, repeated false starts to 'If It's In You', when Barrett tries and fails, and wails his way through the 20-note 'Yes, I'm thi-i-i-nking...'* Waters interjects from the control room, 'Syd, how about tuning the guitar down...' But Barrett stutters back: 'No, it's just the fact of going through it. I mean if we could just cut...' On the other hand, it is thanks to Waters and Gilmour that *Madcap* exists at all.

EMI had run out of patience with Barrett – three weeks' solid sessions were too long for a chaotic, half-finished album – and they were threatening to pull the plug. As for Jones, he had a record label to run, and it was time to bow out honourably. A meeting was arranged with Barrett's old colleagues Waters and Gilmour – now stablemates at Harvest – who agreed to finish the album in a matter of days, squeezing some sessions with Barrett into their ever-tighter schedules.

Between June and August, Gilmour and Waters managed three full days, spread over five sessions. 'We almost laughed our way through it,' says Waters. 'It was so sad and difficult that we had to detach in order to get

* Certainly not David Bowie, who has his own zany studio chat on the album *Hunky Dory* with a 'spontaneous' stoned discussion about the pronunciation of 'Warhol'.

through.' Gilmour remembers that they took a no-nonsense approach: 'Come on, Syd. What have you got? Let's get it down, then.' Waters adds, 'If you were being lovey-dovey, you'd have taken Syd home and tucked him up in bed.' But why mix in the glitches and bum notes and fluffs? Gilmour is still troubled: 'Perhaps we were trying to show what Syd was really like, but perhaps we were trying to punish him.' Waters is dogmatic: 'We wanted something real, like when Joe Cocker's voice cracks at the end of "You Are So Beautiful". It's so full of feeling.'

As are the lyrics. 'Trip, trip to a dream dragon,' Barrett sings in 'Octopus'. 'Hide your wings in a ghost tower,/ Sails crackling at every plate we break.' Whatever else, he has momentum, vision. 'Please hold on to the steel rail'; 'I borrowed a page/From the leopard's cage/And I prowled in the evening sun's glaze': images flash across the mind's eye. Sometimes Barrett seems paranoid: 'It's no good holding your sequinned fan/Where I can't see/because I understand/That you're different from me.'

More often he seems to be attempting some sort of self-analysis: 'When I live I die'; 'Inside me I feel/Alone and unreal'. His most famous lines are probably from 'Dark Globe': 'My head kissed the ground./I was half the way down./Treading the sand./ Please. Please... / Please lift a hand./I'm only a person,/ With Eskimo chain/I tattooed my brain all the way./Won't you miss me?/Wouldn't you miss me at all?'

Not much. For the rest of that summer, the Floyd were busy, so Barrett took a repeat trip to Formentera. He stayed three weeks with an old Cambridge friend, Mary Wing, and her hippie partner, the French artist Marc Dessier. They remember a gentle soul, not much interested in drugs, 'a bit childish, like a little brother who needed looking after'. Did he act weird? 'Listen,' says Dessier, 'many people were weird in those days. Sometimes Syd would speak in non sequiturs, like a kid. He also followed me like a shadow, one metre behind – though he would always push to the front for photographs. But that's not very weird.'

Barrett was on good form, doing handstands on the beach. He looked amazing in tight red cords, Chelsea boots and a silver shirt with puffed sleeves (pinched from Dessier). And if, in private, he seemed hurt by his break with Pink Floyd, in public, on the pull, he claimed he was still in the band – 'which didn't mean much to these European hippie girls, who had never heard of them'. He also began to write, and Dessier has a unique memory of Barrett at work: 'He borrowed my guitar. Then he sat there, chose a letter of the alphabet and thought of his three favourite words starting with the same letter. He wrote them on three bits of paper, threw them in the air and wrote them again in the order that he picked them up. Then, he just kind of filled in the rest. He had given himself a structure.'

Back in London that autumn, Gilmour fitted in two final half-days on *Madcap*. He found the album's name in the lyrics of 'Octopus': 'I wanted him to come across as a jester, not as stark, raving mad.' Barrett looked after the cover, whose organisation was charged to Storm and Po, now the Floyd's art directors. Mick Rock was commissioned to take a photograph, and turned up at Earls Court Square to discover that Barrett had piled his mattress and few possessions against the wall and painted the dusty, unprimed floorboards alternately blue and orange – 'literally painting himself into a corner'. Iggy, after putting kohl on both their eyes, was wondering around the room naked – a typical family scene. Rock fitted a wide lens and, from a single roll of film, captured one of the coolest album sleeves of all time. (It would later win him a place as Bowie's court photographer.) But the credit has to be Barrett's. As Gilmour says, 'Some parts of his brain were still brilliant.'

***

Some, alas, were not. Life in the Earls Court Square flat had started peaceably enough. 'Syd was often charming,' says Fields. Gala recalls Barrett would either be broke or find fifty quid: ' "Here, I've got fifty quid," he'd say. But he might spend the whole lot on biscuits, bread, jam and baked beans – which he ate cold.' At first, Fields was only mildly disconcerted by his flatmate's behaviour. Barrett once drove his Mini the wrong way up the length of the adjoining main road, and later swapped the little car for a friend's enormous Pontiac – which he left untaxed in the street, 'Please Clean Me' etched by finger in the grimy paintwork, until it was towed or given away. He began to keep drawn the green curtains borrowed from his mum, and made the room darker by pinning another layer on top. Then he set fire to the kitchen, cooking chips.

Unable to open his windows, he made the flat stink. (While he was in the bath, Fields would sneak in and fumble with the fabric to let in some fresh air.) But, says Fields, 'Syd wasn't that bad for the times.' After a row, Fields once went to stay with a friend, 'But she was *much* worse than Syd, and after one night I went home.'

The mentally ill often self-medicate with exactly the wrong antidote – and Barrett's poison was Mandrax, the drug of failure and inarticulacy. Fields had a hairy moment, 'when Syd took four pills and started frothing at the mouth'. But he didn't become really worried until Barrett showed his threatening side. Fields didn't mind him kicking Gala's dog, which would crap around the flat while she was out at work; but he drew the line – 'not that she did' – when Barrett threw Gilly Staples across his room.

Despite the modest progress on *Madcap*, there was a huge well of frustration within Barrett. He would rant at Fields: 'Look at you! You're 23 and you're not famous yet!' (Adding poignantly, 'And I'm already a has-been.') He would bitch about Fields to Gala: 'Calls himself an artist? *He* didn't go to the Camberwell School of Art.' When she was allowed into his room, he might turn on her: 'Who are you? Are you a groupie? You're a groupie!' He began to push, shove and scratch her – seeing how far he could go – and played similar mind-games with Fields, flicking lit fag-ends on the floor for him to pick up. He let Rusty and Greta crash in the hall, because they had become homeless, 'and it all became very unpleasant,' says Fields. 'You'd come across bloodstains... Once he had a fight with a taxi-driver.' Another time, he turned up with his guitar at the Wrights' new flat in Bayswater. 'Rick was out, and I was worried,' remembers Juliet. 'Syd said: "Is the pick-up from here today?" I told him that he'd better try the office.'

Briefly, Barrett neglected his appearance, letting his clothes grow ragged, his hair matted, his stubble unshaved. He was probably bored, as well as ill. By the time *Madcap* was finished, the LP had missed the Christmas market and was held over until January. And though he was writing new material, from 6 October 1969 his only work commitments in nearly five months were an erratic guitar session for the ex-Soft Machinist Kevin Ayers, which was later wiped, and a few relatively coherent, often amusing, press interviews. Of *Madcap*'s commercial potential, he remarked ungrammatically, 'It's quite nice, but I'd be surprised if it did anything if I were to drop dead.'

On 24 February 1970, Barrett pre-recorded a session for Radio One's *Top Gear* show, backed by Gilmour on bass and Humble Pie's young Jerry Shirley on drums. 'Syd was great that day,' says Gilmour. 'Listen to those perfect double-tracked vocals. He only had three hours for mixing.' He was also reticent, relaying directions to the control room by whispering them first to Gilmour. Still, two days later the threesome – occasionally joined by Rick Wright on keyboards – started on Barrett's next LP, which Gilmour, ever concerned for his old friend, agreed to produce on his days off.

The *Barrett* album was less lively than its predecessor, partly because of the time it took (about 20 sessions over five months). Gilmour adopted the same approach, and usually had Barrett play along to backing tracks. The result, unfortunately, is less raw than *Madcap*. Barrett's nerve ends are less exposed. He could still be the old Syd, knocking off one of his teenage pastiches, 'Bob Dylan Blues', as an out-take: 'I'm a poet,/Don'tcha know it./And the wind,/You can blow it.' But in 'Wined and Dined', there is a terrible, exhausted sadness. Intended for Gala, it could be an epitaph for his undivided self: 'Wined and dined, oh it seems just like a dream./Girl was so kind, kind of love I've never seen./Only last summer,/It's not so long ago./Just last summer./ Now musk winds blow.' In the lift to his flat after the last night of recording, he expressed the only gratitude that he ever would to Gilmour: 'Thanks... Thanks very much.'

He played live once in the summer, at the 'Olympia Extravaganza' in west London, a four-song gig in the foyer which Gilmour remembers as 'quite together', and Shirley as being abruptly ended by a terrified Barrett. He certainly fled when he bumped into Waters in Harrods, leaving behind two huge bags full – possibly fifty quids worth – of sweets. And soon he would run away from London altogether.

First Gala departed for Ely, and without consulting Fields, Barrett let her room to two girls, a boy and their pets. Then, perversely, Barrett claimed he was sick of the chaos at Earls Court Square, where hangers-on were besieging him during his idle hours, and went to stay with Win. By phone, he asked Duggie to tell the groupies to leave. ('And they were scared he might get violent,' says Fields, 'So they did.') Then he called to say he wouldn't be back. He had hooked up with Gala at the Essex house of Humble Pie's Stevie Marriott; while that band was on tour, she was looking after the singer's dogs Achilles and Seamus (later the star of the eponymous Pink Floyd song). He had invited Gala to live with him in Cambridge, where plenty of his friends had already retreated. Here – on trips to Miller's for records, or to Heffers for art materials – he could have some attention when he wanted it, but two minutes away by bike he was back in his childhood lair at Hills Road.

While Gala divided her time between Cambridge and Ely, Barrett set up home in Win's basement – no, make that coal hole. He could have had his old room back, but he wanted to avoid the lodgers staring at him from the gallery over the hall. ('You are a one,' said Win.) It's a horribly claustrophobic space, reached by a six-foot door hinged into the hall's polished floorboards. Down the open wooden steps is an L-shaped room, about eight foot by eight, with a five-foot ceiling that forces one to stoop. Its brick walls painted white, the only light sources are a small window, set partly beneath the level of the back lawn, and a bare fluorescent tube. Here, Barrett surrounded himself with the relics of yesteryear – his record player and albums, his guitars and amps, his books and art portfolios. Looking though the latter, he found the insect pen-and-inks which would adorn the cover of his second solo LP.

Now he declared that, like his father, he wanted to be a doctor. ('Very nice, dear.') Gala found a sales job in the bedding department of Joshua Taylor's. If he was disturbed, she was 'desperate for some kind of stability – and very naive'. On 1 October 1970, they became engaged, going to Antiquarius in London for the ring. They placed an announcement in the local paper, and received presents wrapped for the big day. Win bought them pots and pans, and a soup tureen. A dinner for both families was organised.

Donald, Alan, Ruth and Roe all gathered at Hills Road with Gala's father, sitting in the dining-room while Barrett gave another mythologised performance. After a few attention-seeking 'Ha's' and 'Hmm's', he threw his tomato soup over Gala. 'And no one said anything! They all behaved as if it was entirely normal.'

During the roast pork, he went to an upstairs bathroom. 'Don't worry,' said Roe. 'He's always been a bit odd.' When he returned, he had cut four inches off his hair, so that now it brushed his collar.

And that was only the beginning. Over the next few weeks, Barrett became dangerously obsessed with Gala. Shaven and suited, he would spy on her, lurking in Joshua Taylor's, where he suspected her of having an affair with another sales assistant. He accused her of screwing around with Jerry Shirley, whom she had met in Earls Court Square: 'Who's this drummer, then? Fuck 'im. Is *he* a pop star?' He began to get rough with Gala again. 'What's going on down there? Are you being naughty?' called Win. 'Syd's mum couldn't see it,' says Gala. 'Maybe she didn't want to know.'

Gala decided to spend all her nights in Ely, and soon received a Dear John letter, addressed to 'Miss Pinion', and signed 'RK Barrett'. She returned the ring. The next day, he sent it back with another letter. 'Hi babe,' he wrote – the wedding was on again! – and he signed himself 'Syd'. But by now Gala's nerves were in shreds. In the winter of 1970, she took another Humble Pie dog-sitting job in Essex – this time for Jerry Shirley. Barrett turned up there one dark night, now with a very short haircut, a purple satin jacket and stack heels. 'Is this a rock star's house?' he said. He scared her, argued with her, and was pushed into the night. He is not known to have had a girlfriend since.

Around this time, Barrett was also giving interviews in London to promote his second solo LP, which was released in November. His speech on such occasions had always been verbose and slightly pretentious; now it fell into the laps of journalists eager to push the insanity angle. But, if one burrows through the verbiage, Barrett made a great deal of sense – so long as he rated who he was talking to. With Giovanni Dadomo, he is playful: 'The guy next door to me paints, and he's doing it well – I don't really feel the need.' With *Beat Instrumental*'s Steve Turner he starts in the same way. Cambridge is 'pretty boring, so I cut my hair'; his cellar was 'quite fun – it's a nice place to live, really, under the ground'; pop music is an 'art form – as much as sitting down is'.

But then, he reveals: 'I've often been in love. The last time [with Gala, presumably] it only lasted a few months and at the end of it I almost broke down... I'd love to get married and have kids. The trouble is, I've forgotten how to love. But I don't worry too much. It's something that occurs to me when I feel a bit blue-jeaned – which I don't always feel.' On the other hand, with *Rolling Stone*'s sensationalist Jonathan Greene, he takes the piss: 'Hey man... look up there, can you see the people on the ceiling?' And with *Melody Maker*'s Michael Watts, he sounds absurdly confident. 'I've never really proved myself wrong,' he says. 'I really need to prove myself right.' His speech may be abstracted but its meaning is fairly clear.

Of his ex-colleagues in the Floyd, Barrett remarks to Watts: 'Their choice of material was always very much to do with what they were thinking as architecture students. Rather unexciting people, I would have thought... Maybe they were working their entry into an art school.' On his alleged acid intake: 'Well, I dunno, it doesn't seem to have much to do with the job.' And, when pressed about breakdowns and break-ups: 'I've always thought of going back to a place where you can drink tea and sit on the carpet. I've been fortunate enough to do that.'

At one stage in Watts' interview, he becomes aware of how disconnected he must sound – 'I feel I'm jabbering' – before again picking up the thread. He talks about making another LP, but not playing live, because of the difficulty of finding the right band: 'They'd have to be lively!' – and besides, 'I haven't got any blue jeans.' He jokes that the skinhead group Slade 'would be an interesting thing to hear', and finishes on an upbeat note about his proposed third album: 'I think I shall be able to produce this one myself. I think it was always easier to do that.' But he never did so again.

***

Barrett was out of time now. The ideas which he had prospected had been stolen and adulterated for the teenybopper market. Glam rock, personified by that real sell-out Marc Bolan, was on the horizon. 'Progressive' rock, as now practised by Pink Floyd, was a direction he eschewed – even though he had pioneered it through such vehicles as 'Interstellar Overdrive' and 'Astronomy Domine'. Heavy metal (Black Sabbath, Deep Purple) was beneath him, and watery soul was the standard in a thousand identical discotheques.

The magical years, when catchy pop and more thoughtful rock could coexist in the same chart – in the same song – were over. Barrett fitted as comfortably into the new order as he did into the platform boots and feathered haircuts that were becoming fashionable. In the industry index, where once he had been classified under 'trailblazers', he was now moved to 'eccentrics'. As EMI were to discover, he would soon be redesignated a cult hero. It's nice – if probably wrong – to think that this was his plan all along.

He spent the rest of 1971 in seclusion, while his legend grew – which is less than can be said for the Gausdens' garden. Visiting Libby's mother, he was asked to cut some flowers, and took out the whole rose crop. He made no music and gave only one interview in the late summer – his last – to Mick Rock, who also photographed him for *Rolling Stone*. It's a good, revealing, insightful piece of writing, and deserves to be quoted at length. 'Syd doesn't see many people these days,' begins Rock. 'Visiting him is like intruding into a very private world…'

> 'I'm disappearing,' he says, 'avoiding most things.' He seems very tense, ill at ease. Hollow-cheeked and pale, his eyes reflect a permanent state of shock. He has a ghostly beauty which one normally associates with poets of old. His hair is short now, uncombed, the wavy locks gone. The velvet pants and new green snake-skin boots show some attachment to the way it used to be. 'I'm treading the back-

ward path,' he smiles. 'Mostly, I just waste my time.' He walks a lot. 'Eight miles a day,' he says. 'It's bound to show. But I don't know how.

'I'm sorry I can't speak very coherently,' he says, 'It's rather difficult to think of anybody being really interested in me. But you know, man, I am totally together. I even think I should be.' Occasionally, Syd responds directly to a question. Mostly his answers are fragmented, a stream of consciousness… 'I'm full of dust and guitars,' he says. 'The only work I've done the last two years is interviews. I'm very good at it.' In fact, Syd… still paints. Sometimes crazy jungles of thick blobs. Sometimes simple linear pieces. His favourite is a white semi-circle on a white canvas…

'All I wanted to do as a kid [was to] play a guitar properly and jump around. But too many people got in the way. It's always been too slow for me. Playing. The pace of things. I mean, I'm a fast sprinter. The trouble was, after playing in the group for a few months, I couldn't reach that point…' Syd leaves the cellar and goes up to a sedate little room full of pictures of himself with his family. He was a pretty child. English tea, cake and biscuits, arrives. Like many innovators, Barrett seems to have missed the recognition due to him, while others have cleaned up.

'I'd like to be rich. I'd like a lot of money to put into my physicals and to buy food for all my friends...'

Syd is 25 now, and worried about getting old. 'I wasn't always this introverted,' he says, 'I think young people should have a lot of fun. But I never seem to have any.' Suddenly he points out the window. 'Have you seen the roses? There's a whole lot of colours.' Syd says he doesn't take acid any more, but he doesn't want to talk about it... 'There's really nothing to say.' He goes into the garden and stretches out on an old wooden seat. 'Once you're into something...' he says, looking very puzzled. He stops. 'I don't think I'm easy to talk about. I've got a very irregular head. And I'm not anything that you think I am anyway.'

What was he, then? At first, he still had some musical ambitions. Through Jenny Spires, who had also retreated to Cambridge, he met her husband Jack Monck, a bass player active in the local scene. Monck suggested that Barrett jam with him and his friend Twink, latterly the drummer with Tomorrow (and later with the Pink Fairies). They played a couple of low-key boogies in January 1972: for the Cambridge Blues Society at the King's College Cellars, and at the Corn Exchange,

Above: Gala Pinion strikes a Seventies pose

Above: Barrett dogsits at Stevie Marriott's Essex home, 1970
Right: a bedraggled publicity shot for *The Madcap Laughs*, 1969

Above: Barrett reveals a new haircut, 1972
Right: attempting a glam-rock image during his last recording sessions, 1974

Barrett benchmarks. *Above*: wearing two pairs of shades in London, 1965
Above right: in Win's garden, 1981. *Right*: Cambridge memorial, 2001

It's awfully considerate of you to think of me here ...
Placed by friends of The Piper /E\ for RKB

MMP Cambridge

Above: Barrett returns from a shopping trip, 2001
- wrapped up warmly, contrary to neighbours' reports

supporting a jazz-and-verse event fronted by two ex-members of Cream, the poet Pete Brown (who had provided lyrics to the group) and the bassist Jack Bruce. When Brown dedicated one of his poems to Barrett – 'because he's here in Cambridge and he's one of the greatest songwriters in the country' – the now-bearded dedicatee shouted from the audience: 'No, I'm not.' However, everyone had been impressed by his still obvious ability, and he was cajoled into forming the Stars with Twink and Monck.

In the Hills Road basement, the Stars rehearsed, among other Barrett numbers, 'Dark Globe' and 'Octopus'. It was, said Twink, 'a pleasure'. They played two free concerts – at the Dandelion café and, open-air, in the Market Square, until the police pulled the plug – and, buoyed by their reception, Twink hustled the new band a slot on the Corn Exchange bill of 24 February, closing for the American rockers MC5. The rumour of Barrett's 'comeback' reached *Melody Maker*, who arranged for it to be reviewed by one Roy Hollingworth.

It couldn't have been at a worse time. While Barrett – clean-shaven again – had been noodling about, his old band had been going from strength to strength, making several albums and selling huge numbers of them in Europe. At London's Rainbow theatre, for four nights in mid-February, the Floyd showcased the piece that was to lift them from fame to superstardom – *The Dark Side of the Moon* – and, on at least one occasion, Barrett was there to watch. It was a tough act to follow, and at the Corn Exchange he failed singularly. 'You could tell Syd just wasn't interested,' says Monck. The PA's mix was so bad that Barrett couldn't hear his own voice, and the bass kept fading out. He only spoke twice, to introduce 'Octopus' and to remark that he couldn't remember the name of 'Gigolo Aunt'. His guitar playing was pathetic, and he cut his finger.

Barrett's old friend Clive Welham was one of the punters who stayed to the end – 'The audience were applauding out of sympathy,' he says – while Hollingworth tried being cruel to be kind. His review is doubtless overdramatised, but it still makes grim reading:

> He played a demented solo that ran ragged lines of up to ten minutes. His raggled hair fell over a face that fell over a guitar and seldom looked up. He changed time almost by the minute, the keys and chords made little sense. The

fingers on his left hand met the frets like strangers. They formed chords, reformed them – apparently nearly got it right – and then wandered away again. Then Syd scratched his nose and let loose a very short sigh. It was like watching somebody piece together a memory that had suffered the most severe shell shock. I don't know how much Syd Barrett remembered, but he didn't give in. Even though he lost his bassist, and even though Twink couldn't share Syd's journey, Syd played on.

The chords are out of tune and he keeps looking to his right and sort of scowling at Twink and the bassist, as though in disagreement. I stood and watched and thought he was bloody great. A girl gets up on stage and dances; he sees her, and looks faintly startled. As the clock ticked into the small hours of Friday morning, Syd retreated to the back of the stage trying to find one of those runs. He messes chords together. There is no pattern but if you think hard you can see a faint one, you can see some trailers in the sky. The large concrete floor is littered now, plastic cups that contained orange juice or lemon or coffee. And some squashed wholenut scones and buns. And underground papers. And Syd played on. Will anyone listen to the Madcap?

When Barrett saw the review the next week, his public reaction was to storm round to Twink's flat and tell him that he had left the Stars. His private reaction was more painful. He went berserk at Hills Road, frightening Win, smashing furniture and bashing his head into the cellar's softboard ceiling.

Cambridge had proved a harder place for hiding than Barrett thought. When Peter Wynne-Wilson dragged him out for a drink, 'he was fairly jumpy, so I took him back home'. When 'the Master' was in town, Susie Gawler-Wright went with Barrett to one of the guru's lectures – but he ran out on being recognised by a member of the audience. A few months before, Jenny Lesmoir-Gordon had unwisely turned the then straight Barrett back on to dope. Bumping into her at a garden centre, he now showed no recognition of her. When Sue Kingsford and some friends were driving up Hills Road, they saw Barrett standing on the kerb. 'What are you up to, Syd?' she said. 'Waiting for a lift,' he replied. 'Well you've got one. Hop in.' They went to a nearby pub, 'and Syd didn't say a word.'

Nor did he write one. Yet, in the wake of Pink Floyd's enormous success, his finances prospered. *Relics*, a 1971 compilation album, was delivering ample royalties and Barrett – by now a little overweight – began regular visits to London, where he would pick up cheques from Bryan Morrison, the entrepeneur who also owned Barrett's music-publishing company. At first, he stayed at the Park Lane Hilton. Then, pleased with the new type of anonymity offered by the capital, in 1974 he rented a couple of two-room flats in Chelsea Cloisters, a serviced apartment block in the no-man's-land between Sloane Square and South Kensington. He lived on the ninth floor, in room 902, and kept all his equipment – to which he regularly added – on the sixth. 'If John Lennon can have two homes, so can I,' he said on one of his cheque-runs to Lupus Music, when the staff chided him about his extravagance.

Cora Barnes was the lady in charge of accounts at Lupus, responsible for ensuring that Barrett signed the register after each payment. One day, she was surprised to see him appear, as he had only been in for a cheque the day before. 'No I wasn't,' said Barrett. She showed him the register, which he had signed with a red pen. 'You're ripping me off!' he screamed. 'I would never sign anything with a red pen!' Hearing the commotion,

Morrison appeared from his inner sanctum and began to tell Barrett what for. Seizing his jabbing finger, Barrett bit it as hard as he could – to the bone, in fact – and drew a swell of blood. He was subsequently barred from the Lupus office.

While Win sold the Cambridge family home and moved south-west – to a two-bedroomed house in the faceless suburban terraces of Cherry Hinton – Barrett reinstalled himself in the capital, buying a wide-screen television and a white 'egg' chair that hung from a chain on the ceiling (or possibly the other way round). Again he drew and fixed the curtains. His old friends would sometimes still visit, but they felt unwelcome and uneasy.

Apart from watching TV and eating a great deal – aggravating the beginnings of a stomach ulcer – Barrett's life largely consisted of walks to and from the Marlborough, a local pub which served good Guinness. One apocryphal tale has a friend seeing him striding down Oxford Street and, upset by being ignored, asking Barrett where he was going in such a hurry. 'Far further than you could possibly imagine,' was the supposed reply. Another has him visiting a King's Road shop, trying on three pairs of trousers in different sizes, and buying the lot.

He could afford to. The recent repackaging of the first two Floyd LPs as a double-album – and Bowie's cover of 'Emily' on his tribute-album *Pin Ups** – had made him richer than ever before. More royalties were on the way from the re-release of his solo LPs as a double-album set. He began to indulge in absurd acts of generosity. Taking a porter, Ronnie Salmon, to his sixth-floor storeroom, he removed some guitars and gave the rest of the lumber – amps, portable televisions, records and tapes – to Salmon. And soon he extended his largesse to anyone waiting on him: porters received gifts of stereo equipment; a hi-fi delivery man left with a £300 tip.

Intoxicated by the disposability of disposable culture, Barrett bought suits and shirts, wore them for a day, then threw them away. Like his own imitator David Bowie, he began to experiment with ambiguous 'images': shaving

* Bowie had also reached superstar status by now, with his 1972 album *Ziggy Stardust*. The character of Ziggy was originally conceived as a transvestite 'discovered' by Bowie and called Arnold Korns, in homage to Barrett's Arnold Layne. Though Bowie changed his character's name after hearing 'The Legendary Stardust Cowboy', a loopy one-hit wonder called Norman Odam – and though he later claimed that the mad rocker Vince Taylor was his inspiration – the 'rock'n'roll suicide' Ziggy bears many resemblances to Barrett: 'He came on so loaded, man./Well-hung and snow-white tan.'

his head again, and bleaching the regrown hair; walking the streets in a dress. Whether he was playing with people, or laughing at them, no one will ever know. But sometimes the old rage resurfaced: once, he smashed his flat door off its hinges. So his recovery clearly had some way to go.

Unfortunately, he still had commercial potential. EMI, pleasantly surprised by the sales of his re-released albums and insistent on their 1968 contract, told Jenner to take Barrett back into Abbey Road. He was corralled into four days' sessions, but they were a waste of time. 'He didn't really want to be there,' says the studio engineer John Leckie. Barrett tried to bite the hand of a studio asssistant, who waved a red-printed piece of paper at him. (Did he think it was a bill?) He had no words, no tunes, and, after several pointless jams, the enterprise was abandoned. Barrett would never record again, nor enter Abbey Road – except on one legendary occasion.

After 18 months of touring, writing and rehearsing, the Floyd had returned to the studio. By June 1975 – with a three-week US tour looming, and Gilmour disappearing for his wedding the next month – they were putting the finishing touches to *Dark Side*'s sequel, *Wish You*

Were Here. The whole album sprang from a haunting – haunted – four-note guitar phrase of Gilmour's, which had then inspired Waters' memorial to Barrett, 'Shine On You Crazy Diamond'. On 5 June, they were fiddling about on the mixing-desk, in the room overlooking Studio Three. 'A very fat man dressed in white was messing about in the studio,' remembers Gilmour. He had a shaved head and, possibly, shaved eyebrows. But who was the first to spot Barrett? And did he come on subsequent days? Did he go up to the control room before or after Gilmour's sighting? And who else saw him? It's a critical moment in the Barrett myth – yet no one can quite remember the details.

Rick Wright says Barrett was sitting on the control-room sofa, jumping up and down to clean his teeth; strapping on a guitar and asking if it was his turn yet. (Hmmm, as the Barrett-admiring writer Nick Kent would say.) Gilmour and Waters are hazy. Plenty of people who weren't there swear they were and display wondrous examples of false-memory syndrome. It's possible that Barrett heard 'Shine On' if the band were working on it that day – so he may have said, 'Sounds a bit old.' If they replayed the track, he conceivably could have said, 'Why bother? You've heard it once already.' But no one knows. His sister Roe once claimed the whole visit was a practical joke which backfired. And to put a final dampener on the story, Gilmour points out: 'When we'd last been in London for any length of time, we'd seen a bit of Syd. I don't know if it was *that* unusual.'

By now, the Syd Barrett Appreciation Society (founded in 1972) had folded, due to 'lack of Syd'. But he wasn't quite invisible. In 1977, Gala Pinion was in the Europa supermarket on the Fulham Road, a few hundred yards from the Cloisters. As she went in, she felt sure she recognised the short-haired, flabby man paying at the till; he was dressed in a pinstripe suit and white shirt, 'like the doctor he'd wanted to be'. When she came out, Barrett was waiting for her on the street. 'Where are you going, then?' he said. 'I'm going to buy you a drink.' They went for a half of Guinness to the Marlborough, and he invited her back to his flat. Once there, 'He dropped his trousers and pulled out his cheque book,' says Pinion. 'How much do you want?' he asked. 'Come on, get your knickers down.'

Gala made her excuses and left, never to see him again. However, even as an invisible presence, he loomed large. The previous year, punk rock had appeared and the King's Road had become its heartland. Without success, the Sex Pistols, their manager Malcolm McLaren and their art director Jamie Reid tried to contact Barrett, to ask him to produce their first album.* The Damned hoped he would produce their second, realised it was impossible and settled for the Floyd's Nick Mason (who 'didn't have a clue', according to the band's bassist Captain Sensible).

Barrett continued to do as little and spend as much as ever. Bankrupt, he left London for Win's new Cambridge home in 1981.

***

An operation on his ulcer meant that Barrett lost much of his excess weight. Win thought he should keep himself occupied, so Roger Waters' mother Mary found him a gardening job with some wealthy friends. At first he prospered but, during a thunderstorm, he threw down his

* The band's second bassist, the late John Ritchie, may have chosen the name Sid Vicious in honour of Barrett – or of Sid, the hamster belonging to his friend, Johnny Rotten.

tools and left. He made no new friends, and avoided old ones.* He only called himself 'Roger' now. In 1982, his finances restored, he booked into the Chelsea Cloisters for a few weeks but found he disliked London. He heard the voice of freedom and he followed – *walking* back to Cambridge, where he was found on Win's doorstep – and leaving his dirty laundry behind.

Cue two French journalists from *Actuel* magazine. Arriving at the Cloisters days after Barrett had left, they offered to repatriate his laundry, and took the train to Cambridge. Discovering Barrett's address, the writer and photographer rang the bell...

> 'Hello.'
>
> We're both surprised at the meeting. Our voices tremble slightly.
>
> 'I'm here to bring you your clothes. Do you remember?'
>
> 'Oh yes. In Chelsea. Yes...'
>
> He's an old, tired man. Very short hair, balding at the

* None of the Floyd has talked to him since 1975, because they have been told that Barrett can become upset for a fortnight if he is reminded of their time together. None the less, Gilmour has made sure that all Barrett's royalties reach him, and has sent a unilateral Christmas card for the last few years.

temples, drawn features, glassy-eyed with arms hanging at his sides...

'I've been trying to see you. I went to Chelsea. They told me that there was some washing and that you live with your mother.'

'Thanks very much,' he says. 'Do you want some money. Did they make you pay?'

'No, really, it's all right. What do you do now? Do you paint?'

'No. I've just had an op, but it's nothing serious. I'm trying to get back [to London] but there's a train strike at the moment.' [There wasn't.]

'What do you do in your London flat? Do you play your guitar?'

'No, I watch TV, that's all.'

'Don't you want to play any more?'

'No, not really. I'll have to find myself a new flat there, but it's difficult. I'll have to wait.' Now and again, he looks at his washing, he fidgets, he smiles. 'I didn't think I'd get these things back, and I knew I couldn't write for them. I didn't get around to deciding to go back for them. Mum told me she'd ring the office. Thanks all the same...'

'Can I take a photo of you?'

'Yes, of course.' He smiles, stands to attention and smartens his collar. 'Good, that's it now, thanks.' He looks at the tree outside his house. I don't know what else to say.

'That tree's lovely.'

'Yes, but not now. They trimmed it not long ago. Before, I really liked it.'

At the back of the house his mum speaks: 'Roger, come and have a cup of tea and say hello to my friends.' Roger turns towards me, panicked.

'Mmm, good, okay. Perhaps we'll see each other in London. Goodbye.'

And good riddance? From then until now, only a handful of encounters with Barrett have been reported first-hand, but some facts have come to light. The circumstances of his final return to Cambridge were rightly interpreted by his family as a 'cry for help', and he agreed to spend a spell in Fulbourne psychiatric hospital. (It has often been said that Barrett developed schizophrenia. In fact, neither diagnosis nor medication has ever been offered, on the grounds that he has an 'odd' mind, rather than a sick one.) He continued for a while as an outpatient at Fulbourne, catching the yellow bus there on his own, with no trouble.

Barrett has never been sectioned. He has never had to take drugs for his mental health, except after one or two uncontrollable fits of anger, when he was admitted to Fulbourne and administered Largactyl. However, he has received other treatments. In the early Eighties, he spent two years in a charitable institution, Greenwoods, in Essex. At this halfway-house for lost souls, he joined in group and other forms of therapy, and was very content. But after an imagined slight, he walked out – again, all the way to his mother's house. The increasingly frail Win moved in with Roe and her husband, according to Mary Waters, 'because she was so scared of his outbursts'.

Strange, then, that he could still crack jokes about 'buying a ticket for the yellow bus'. But Barrett's behaviour has remained pleasingly unpredictable. Mick Rock was surprised, when he wrote asking for a signature on the 'release-form' for his Seventies pictures, that 'Syd returned it, signing himself RK Barrett'. Libby Gausden ran into him in the Cherry Hinton supermarket in 1985, 'And he was on great form. He had the right style for the times – the right jeans, the right T-shirt, even if he was looking miles away. But he was carrying one of those old ladies' maroon and cream plastic shopping bags. When he was a teenager, if Rog had seen someone like himself, cycling round Cambridge with his little bag, he'd have made a joke about it. I told him he was just like one of the people he used to write about – like Arnold Layne – and he threw back his head and roared with laughter. He said, "It's ridiculous, I know, but I have to do the shopping every day." Then my husband came up, and Rog clammed up completely.'

Some people think Barrett suffers from Asperger's Syndrome. It certainly seems he can't be bothered to think about anything that doesn't directly affect him. He kept rabbits and cats for a while but forgot to feed them, so they had to be sent to more caring homes. Thereafter the only intimate contacts he maintained were with Win and Roe. Otherwise, he seems to have lost the habit – and become wary – of human interaction, limiting himself to encounters with shop assistants and his sympathetic GP, whose surgery has become a second home. He was – and is still – in and out of hospital for his ulcers.

The clamour from Barrett obsessives has hardly let up in three decades. The late Malcolm Jones published a

Above: detail from the Floyd's first album-cover
Following pages: cover and extracts from Barrett's 'magazine', *Fart Enjoy*

FART
ENJOY

LIEUTENANT LUNCH-DATE TURNED BACK FROM HIM FEELING OF WARM

STAGE ACTS HAVE BECOME IMPORTANT WHOSO DIGGETH A PIT SHALL

FALL THEREIN THEY EVEN DEFENDED BRITISH POP PRINCES OF THE KINGDOM

OF BABYLON SUCH A TERRIBLE FEELING OF INADEQUECY SWEEPS IN A CURVE

THUS SAITH THE LORD GOD SEX SYMBOL GOOD MADE DEATH UNTO ME?

DANK CORRIDOORS HEAR POP ENTRIES ASHAMED IN THIS SAME CONFIDENT

BOASTING MORTAL BLOWN KNOBBY SLABS OF WHITE STONE RUBBLE ITS

BEGINNING TO AFFECT OUR EAR-DRUMS TONY CARTWRIGHT AND TOM

JONES YOU CAN BANK ON THIS JUNGLE PRINT DRESS GOING STRAIGHT

TO

HIS

HEART.

HARK! JACK WAS DIDDLTY DUMPTY

ALL JOLL

TO MARKET TO BUY A PLUM CAKE

crowaves?
E POST OFFICE
TOWER
Why
so tall
volving
taurant
WAS BUILT
EXAMPLE, ONE OF THE LIGHT
CHANNELS SUCH NEAR
WAVELENGTHS AND THEIR FREQUENC
SUBSTANTIALLY BE
"FREQUENCY" EXTREMELY A
THEY TO OBSERVATION
LIGHT SO
LIGHT, I.E. THEY TRAVEL IN
WAVELENGTHS AERIALS LTD.
BEHAVE ITSELF
ONE BE REVOLVING
PER SECOND MICROWAVE RADIO SI
LIGHT ALL COCKTAIL
FREQUENCY EXTREMELY A
FREQUENCY EXTREMELY
"FREQUENCY" AS APPLIED TO A
SUBSTANTIALLY BE
MOST OF THE
OF A TOP
OF RADIO, MOST PEOPLE ARE.

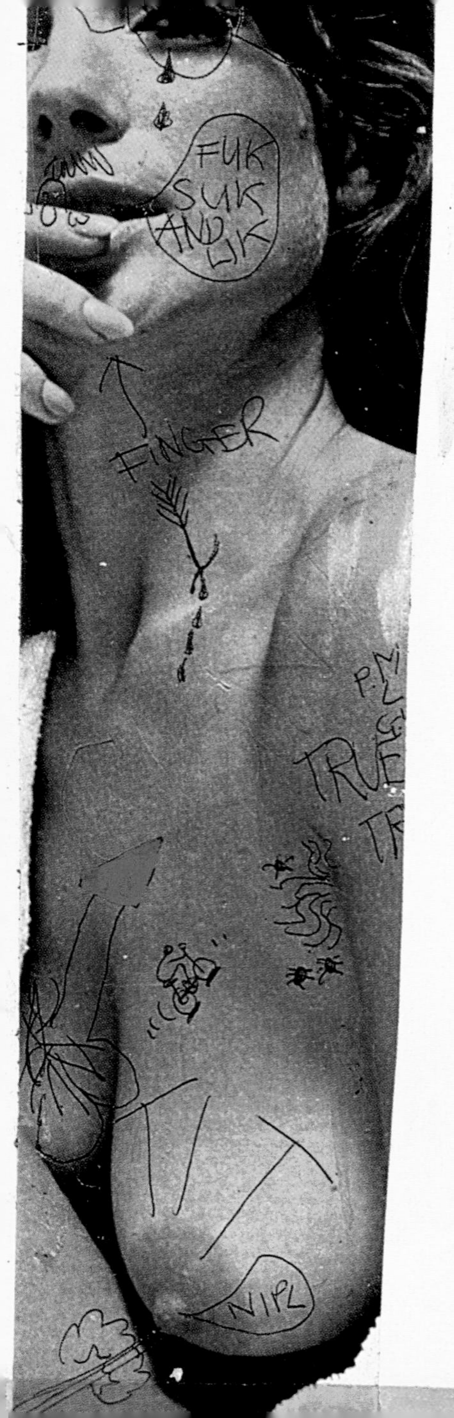


```
B O Y S     F U C
B O Y   F S   U C
B O   F Y U S   C
B   F O U Y C S
F   B U O C Y K
F U   B C O K   Y
F U C   B K   O Y
F U C K     B O Y
F U C K     B O Y
F U C K     B O   G
F U C K     B   G C
F U C K     G   B I
F U C K     G I   F
F U C K     G I R
F U C K     G I R L
```

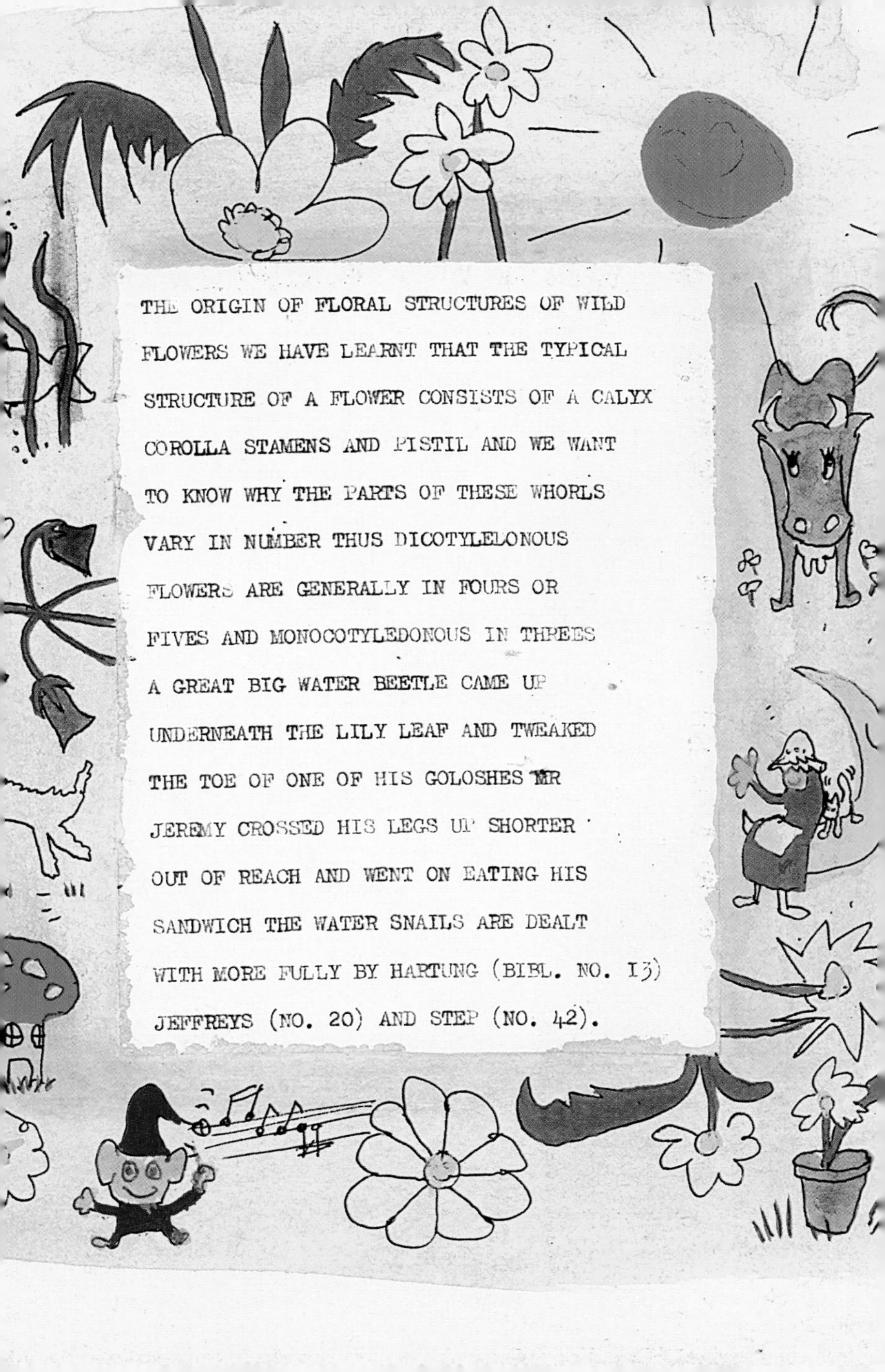

THE ORIGIN OF FLORAL STRUCTURES OF WILD FLOWERS WE HAVE LEARNT THAT THE TYPICAL STRUCTURE OF A FLOWER CONSISTS OF A CALYX COROLLA STAMENS AND PISTIL AND WE WANT TO KNOW WHY THE PARTS OF THESE WHORLS VARY IN NUMBER THUS DICOTYLEDONOUS FLOWERS ARE GENERALLY IN FOURS OR FIVES AND MONOCOTYLEDONOUS IN THREES A GREAT BIG WATER BEETLE CAME UP UNDERNEATH THE LILY LEAF AND TWEAKED THE TOE OF ONE OF HIS GOLOSHES MR JEREMY CROSSED HIS LEGS UP SHORTER OUT OF REACH AND WENT ON EATING HIS SANDWICH THE WATER SNAILS ARE DEALT WITH MORE FULLY BY HARTUNG (BIBL. NO. 13) JEFFREYS (NO. 20) AND STEP (NO. 42).

Left: Barrett crouches for the cover of his first solo album

Right: the teenage Barrett's ink sketches of insects adorn his second solo album-cover

privately printed booklet in 1986, recording his memories of the *Madcap* sessions, and detailing which tracks and alternative takes remained in the vaults. Armed with this knowledge, hardcore fans petitioned EMI for their release, and the result was the *Opel* album, a dubious addition to the Barrett canon, containing the eponymous, awful title-track, a version of the tedious 'Lanky', and various out-takes that would better have remained buried. The year before, five tracks from the excellent Radio One recordings of 1970 had been released. Now, to coincide with *Opel*, the DJ Nicky Horne put together a tribute programme for the same station, featuring an interview with Roe's husband.

Paul Breen revealed that his brother-in-law was 'painting again', and meeting his mother in town for twice-weekly shopping trips. It was a 'very, very ordinary lifestyle,' said Breen, but not reclusive: 'I think the word "recluse" is probably emotive. It would probably be truer to say that he enjoys his own company now, rather than that of others.'

As for his heyday, 'I think it's a part of his life which he prefers to forget now. He had some bad experiences and thankfully has come through the worst of these, and is able – fortunately – to lead a normal life in Cambridge.' And regarding his state of mind: 'There's a level of contentment now which he probably hasn't felt since before he got involved in music, in fact. He is developing new interests, and particularly his painting – which has progressed as the years go by.'

As more years went by, other news leaked out. Barrett was collecting coins. He was learning to cook, and could stuff a mean pepper. On the death of Win in 1991, he had destroyed all his old diaries and art books – and also chopped down the front garden's fence and tree, and burned them (though more in a spirit of renewal than grief). He had been a great support to Roe in her mourning, but hadn't attended the funeral because he 'wouldn't know what to do'. He still wrote down his thoughts all the time. He still painted – big works, six foot by four – but destroyed any that he didn't consider perfect, and stacked the rest against the wall. As with 'Emily', he lost interest in things once they were finished. And sometimes he was unable to finish them, because obsessive fans had climbed over his back fence, and stolen the brushes from the table outside, where he worked. (One guilty individual recalls a canvas in orange and red.)

He lived for the day, which meant that Roe had to keep an eye on his tomorrows, and was unable to take long holidays. He had a short attention-span, which ruled out most television-watching – though he liked programmes with a heavy factual content. He delighted in the dahlias at Anglesey Abbey, near Lode, and had shelves full of glossy gardening books. He enjoyed visiting Cambridge's art galleries on his own, and twice took the train to the Tate in London. (The second time, he lost his ticket home and Roe had to send a taxi for him.) His spending money was controlled by Alan, because he had gained no more financial nous than that displayed at Chelsea Cloisters. He didn't converse, so much as make statements – another symptom of Asperger's. Being childish in that way, he got on best with children. He was passionate about, if hopeless at, DIY. He was a gent, always walking on the outside when he and Roe went shopping in town. He talked to her every day on the phone.

On the musical front, several names expressed an interest in recording with him, including Jimmy Page and Brian Eno* – an Ipswich native, who had met Barrett in

* Eno, of course, saved David Bowie's career, producing *Low* in 1977 for the then drug-befuddled Bowie.

his teens. In 1992, his post-Floyd albums were put out as a boxed CD set, with several more out-takes included as 'bonus tracks'. And, in the same year, Atlantic Records allegedly offered him £75,000 to record whatever he wanted, with whoever he pleased, in his kitchen if necessary. They didn't hear back. But in 1994, Barrett made a surprise approach to someone.

Libby Gausden's daughter Abigail – then a student at Cambridge University – was 'walking to lectures at Sedgwick from St Catharine's, when this bald man on a bike pulled up to the kerb'. Abigail was wearing one of her mother's old coat-dresses, a black and yellow patterned number from Barbara Hulanicki, which Libby had bought after meeting Biba's founder at the Festival Hall 30 years before. 'Hello, little Lib,' said Barrett. 'Hello,' said Abigail blithely, and moved on. 'It was a few seconds before I realised what he had called me,' she recalls. 'Then a friend said, "Do you know that was Syd Barrett?" I turned round and he was gone.'

But not forgotten. In 1996, Barrett's 23-year-old nephew by Donald gave an email interview to an Internet Syd-site. As well as repeating many of Paul Breen's sentiments, Ian Barrett revealed that Barrett owned an acoustic guitar and 'a little record player', and described his uncle's recent paintings: 'He's been very interested in geometric patterns and repeated shapes; the kind of things you might see in tiles and weaving. I've seen abstracts in oils, naturalistic watercolours, wood-block work.' Most fascinating of all, Ian disclosed that Barrett had been 'writing a book, purely for his own enjoyment, about the history of art... I doubt very much he would ever want it published, but he's used a word-processor to put it together, and I assume it's brought him a lot of pleasure.'

Ian grew up in Luton, where his father worked. It was family lore, he said, that in the Seventies Barrett had stayed in his basement, avoiding visitors. Even now, 20 years later, he was unable to cope with large gatherings. However, Ian added, Barrett had visited Donald in Luton several times, just for the day – once in the early Eighties at Christmas, when Ian had showed him how to play tunes on one of his presents, an electronic toy. He described Barrett's manner of speech as 'strange and fragmented... so everyday things come out sounding quite abstract, but it all has its own internal logic and it's just his way of expressing himself'.

On the acid question, following the Barrett family line, Ian said: 'I have absolutely no idea what his views on drugs are now; but I don't really think that it takes much imagination to work out what his viewpoint might be after all he went through because of them.' And on a personal note, he added that 'what really makes me sick... is the way he is written off as a madman – a rock genius who was just such a crazed madcap that there is no need to worry about the extent of pain and anguish he went through... Without going into details, I don't think people are prepared to understand the true extent of Roger's breakdown or the pressures he was put under.'

Still the Barrett industry grew. Later that year, a one-man show about him premiered at the ICA in London; early the next, the Blur guitarist Graham Coxon exhibited a sculpture dedicated to him – the latest in a long line of musicians to doff their caps. In fact, Barrett had remained an icon among musos ever since the days of punk. In 1982, the Boomtown Rats were still performing 'Arnold Layne'. Such diverse talents as Julian Cope of Teardrop Explodes, Robert Smith of the Cure, Paul Weller of the Jam and Siouxsie of the Banshees have all acknowledged his influence. Following Kevin Ayers' 1972 song, 'Oh! Wot a Dream', the Television Personalities and Robyn Hitchcock have also recorded tributes to Barrett – Hitchcock rather desperately trying to reincarnate himself as the Piper.

On record, Barrett has been covered by dozens of artists, among them Marc Almond, the Shamen, the Soup Dragons, the Soft Boys, and the Jesus and Mary Chain. On stage, Michael Stipe of REM has chilled crowds with his a cappella version of 'Dark Globe'. The Gilmour-led Pink Floyd has dusted off the band's first-ever album-track – Barrett's 'Astronomy Domine' – while Gilmour himself has tingled spines in his recent solo sets with his covers of 'Terrapin' and 'Dominoes'.

In the last few months, this Barrett activity has shown little sign of abating: a 'Best of' album – *Wouldn't You Miss Me?* – was released, including 'Bob Dylan Blues' as a bonus track. This led a *Daily Mail* photographer to ambush Barrett, who said, 'I think you'd better leave it, I don't do that any more.' A covertly shot video of Barrett walking through Cambridge in the mid-Nineties was offered for sale on the Internet. And Mick Rock published a book of all his Barrett photos in a limited edition of 950 – of which 320 had ruled flyleaves signed 'Barrett' by the man himself. Unsigned, the book costs £195, signed £495 (which is quite cheap, when the Internet claims that a 'Syd Barrett' signature can sell for £6,000). His hand is rounded, less of a scrawl than in his Floyd days. It is understood that Barrett took some persuading, and received a hefty sum for this work. But what is really intriguing is that one part of his brain could work well enough to cut a sweet deal without having to call himself 'Syd' in the process.

A few titbits, to finish. In 1998, Barrett was diagnosed as a B-type diabetic – a genetic condition – and was prescribed a regime of medication and diet, to which he is sporadically faithful. His eyesight will inevitably become 'tunnelled' as a result – sooner, rather than later, unless he regularly takes his tablets. However, he is far from 'blind', as reported on the more excitable websites.

In the winter of 2001, a hard-core group of fans (who call themselves 'Echoes', and use '/E\' as their symbol) paid for a dedicatory bench to be placed in Cambridge, in a location which they have asked to be kept 'secret'. One of their number, an Antipodean called Dion Johnson, knocked on Barrett's door to show him a map of where to find it, and was delighted that his taciturn hero not only asked for a copy of the map, but gave him an 'RK Barrett' autograph. It is not known if Barrett has visited the bench, on which he will find a brass plaque quoting his sarcastic line from 'Jugband Blues': '"It's awfully considerate of you to think of me here..." Placed by friends of the Piper /E\ for RKB.'

For Christmas that year, Barrett gave his sister a painting of the hollyhocks and shed in his back garden. For his birthday in January 2002, she bought him a new stereo, because he likes to listen to the Stones, Booker-T and the classical composers. However, he evinced no interest in the recent *Echoes: The Best of Pink Floyd* (on which nearly a fifth of the tracks are written by him, despite the fact that he only recorded with the band for less than a thirtieth of its lifespan). To coincide with the album's release, the BBC screened an *Omnibus* documentary about him, which he watched round at Roe's house. He is reported to have liked hearing 'Emily' and, particularly, seeing his old landlord Mike Leonard – who he called his 'teacher'. Otherwise, he thought the film 'a bit noisy'.

Brief Encounter (B)

'MISTER Barrett?'

'Yes.'

His voice is deeper than on any recordings, more cockneyfied than on the TV interviews he gave in '67. Behind him, the hall is clean but bare, the floorboards mostly covered in linoleum. I mention someone dear to him, from his childhood. She'd be coming to Cambridge in a couple of weeks, and wondered if Barrett might like a visit?

'No.'

He stands and stares, less embarrassed than me by the vision of him in his underpants.

'So is everything all right?'

'Yeah.'

'You're still painting?'

'No, I'm not doing anything,' he says (which is true –

he's talking to me). 'I'm just looking after this place for the moment.'

'For the moment? Are you thinking of moving on?'

'Well, I'm not going to stay here for ever.' He pauses a split-second, delivers an unexpectedly jaunty 'Bye-bye', and slams the door.

I'm left, like others before me, trying to work out just what he meant. *I'm not going to stay here for ever.* Does he just mean, 'One day, I might move house.' Or is it a nod to the fate that awaits us all? A coded message that he may re-emerge into the world – perhaps show new work or perform? And is opening the door in your underpants an unwitting demonstration of self-confidence, or an eccentricity, or worse? I retrace my steps, cross the main road to my car, where I write a note that I hope is tactful: 'Dear Mr Barrett – I'm sorry to have disturbed your sunbathing. I didn't have time to mention that I'm writing a book on you...' I plead my case, give my telephone number, and return down the cracked tarmac pavement.

As I reach the gate, I see him weeding in the front corner of the garden, on his knees by the new fence. This time, I notice a stump, expertly cross-hatched, and presumably the remains of the tree remarked on by the *Actuel* journalists. 'Hi,' I say. 'I've just written a note to you.'

'Huh,' he says, not looking up, throwing roots behind him.

'May I leave it?' He straightens and stares into my eyes, but doesn't answer. He's wearing khaki shorts now, and gardening gloves, which aren't really suited to receiving the note – and I would be tempting fate to rest it on the side of the wheelbarrow which he has brought with him.

'Shall I put it through the letterbox?'

'It's nothing to do with me,' he says. So I do.

'Nice day,' I say, on leaving. 'Goodbye.'

He doesn't reply, and I never hear from him.

Afterword

IT'S nothing to do with me. Meaning, 'Do what you like'? Or, 'The man you want to interview has nothing to do with me, Roger Barrett'? Or both?

In total, I've spent a few seconds with my subject – yet I'm quite content he's just as sane as me. Roe has said that 'none of this would have happened if it wasn't for the drugs' and, to some extent, she's right. But neither would those compelling solo albums. And compared to other rock'n'roll tragedies, Barrett hasn't come through too badly.

He's well-off from the Floyd's seemingly never-ending royalties. He's not a cokehead; and there are many worse so-called 'acid casualties'. Severe clinical depression invariably encompasses a death wish – but in 30 years there's never been any hint of that. (Indeed, Roe has been reported to say that 'he's always optimistic'.) And, as his old sidekick Mick Rock croaks, 'At least he's not dead.'

I've been thinking about Thoreau's *Walden* recently, and Voltaire's *Il faut cultiver notre jardin*. I've been reminded of Pascal's injunction against curiosity, and the quietism of à Kempis. There has always been a romantic faction of Barrett freaks who think that, after some years of conflicting emotions, their hero chose to walk away from the corruption and tawdriness of the music business, and I side with them. If he tends his garden, perhaps that's because he sees little point in anything else, since the pure, spontaneous creation that he sought was impossible.

Thoreau was the man responsible for that great Sixties poster slogan, 'If a man does not keep pace with his companions, perhaps it is because he hears a different drummer.' To paraphrase him: the arts have no meaning without integrity; the most elevated intercourse is seldom higher than vanity and gossip; fame is a phantom, its game not worth the candle; all work beyond supplying the barest needs of self-sufficiency is self-enslavement; travel narrows the mind, and middlemen are parasites. For this mid-19th century Ur-hippie, the proper object of mankind was meditation and observation. To watch a campfire burn, or a squirrel forage, was entertainment and education enough.

'Please leave us here,' wrote Barrett. 'Close our eyes to the Octopus Ride.' He climbed out of the hurtling fairground wagon, and found his centre in solitude. (Ugh. *People!*) Perhaps the faceless terraced acres of south Cambridge are Barrett's Walden wood, his back garden the clearing where he can rest in peace. He's not going to stay there for ever, he says. But it could be argued that he has survived there for the last 15 years with relatively little hassle from intruders or from his troubles. And what else could he do, except emigrate – and still be tracked down? Besides, why should he run and hide? He's home. Thoreau built his own house, Barrett fixes up his. And if one of Thoreau's critics has protested that his backwoods philosophy was 'of doubtful application to the existence of a wife and children' – well, that's no hurdle to Barrett.

Previous biographers have made much of the woods in the landscape of Barrett's mind. The scarey Wildwood, where Ratty and Mole had their pantheistic vision of the Piper at the Gates of Dawn; the Beech Woods, south of Cambridge, where Barrett took early acid trips. But here's Barrett in 'Octopus' again: 'Isn't it good to be lost in the woods!' And here's Thoreau in *Walden*: 'It is a surprising and memorable, as well as valuable experience, to be lost in the woods... Not till we have lost the world, do we begin to find ourselves, and realise where we are and the infinite extent of our relations.'

Barrett, I'm sure, has realised.

Sketch by Barrett, 1962

BARRETT'S CONCERT AND STUDIO SCHEDULE, 1965-72

Readers who are handy with a map and stopwatch can see from this list – which excludes television appearances – how much pressure Barrett was working under. Between 1965 and 1968, he also moved home five times.

1965

Early February	The Countdown Club, Kensington, London
22 February	Homerton College, Cambridge
27 June	a) Melody Maker National Beat Contest, Wimbledon Palais, London b) Beat Contest, The Country Club, Haverstock Hill, London
Summer	Byam Shaw School of Art, London
Summer	Recording at Regent Sound, Denmark Street, London: 'Lucy Leave', 'King Bee', 'Double-O Bo', 'Untitled'
November	January twins' birthday party, Great Shelford, Cambridgeshire
December	The Goings-On Club, Archer Street, London

1966

9 January	The Goings-On
30 January	The Marquee Club, Wardour Street, London
6 February	The Marquee
27 February	The Marquee
11 March	Essex University
13 March	The Marquee
27 March	The Marquee

3 April	The Marquee
17 April	The Marquee
1 May	The Marquee
8 May	The Marquee
15 May	The Marquee
12 June	The Marquee
September	Banstead Art College
30 September	All Saints Hall, Notting Hill, London
14 October	All Saints Hall
15 October	IT launch party, The Roundhouse, London
21 October	All Saints Hall
28 October	All Saints Hall
31 October	Recording at Thompson Private Recording Studios, Hemel Hempstead: 'Interstellar Overdrive', 'Nick's Boogie'
4 November	All Saints Hall
5 November	a) Wilton Hall, Bletchley b) Five Acres, Bricket Wood, Watford
8 November	All Saints Hall
11 November	All Saints Hall
15 November	All Saints Hall
18 November	Hornsey College of Art
19 November	Technical College, Canterbury
22 November	All Saints Hall
29 November	All Saints Hall
December	Recording at CBC Studios, Great Portland Street, London: 'Interstellar'
3 December	The Roundhouse
12 December	Oxfam benefit, Royal Albert Hall, London
22 December	The Marquee
23 December	UFO, Tottenham Court Road, London
29 December	The Marquee

30 December	UFO
31 December	a) Cambridge Technical College b) The Roundhouse

1967

5 January	The Marquee
6 January	Seymour Hall, London
8 January	The Upper Cut, Forest Gate, London
11 January	Recording at Sound Techniques, Old Church Street, London, two sessions: 'Interstellar', 'Nick's Boogie'
12 January	Sound Techniques: mixing
13 January	UFO
14 January	Reading University
16 January	ICA, London
17 January	Commonwealth Institute, London
19 January	The Marquee
20 January	UFO
21 January	The Birdcage Dancehall, Portsmouth
27 January	UFO
28 January	Essex University
29 January	Sound Techniques: 'Arnold Layne', 'Candy and a Currant Bun'
2 February	Cadenna's, Guildford
3 February	Queens Hall, Leeds
9 February	New Addington Hotel, Croydon
10 February	Leicester College of Technology
11 February	Sussex University
17 February	Dorothy Ballroom, Cambridge
18 February	California Ballroom, Dunstable
20 February	Adelphi Ballroom, West Bromwich

21 February	Recording at EMI Studios, Abbey Road, London: 'Matilda Mother'
23 February	EMI: mixing
24 February	a) The Ricky Tick Club, Windsor b) UFO
25 February	The Ricky Tick, Hounslow
27 February	EMI: 'Interstellar'
28 February	Blaises, Kensington, London
1 March	a) Eel Pie Island Hotel, Twickenham b) EMI: mixing
2 March	Assembly Hall, Worthing
3 March	Market Hall, St Albans
4 March	Regent Street Polytechnic, London
5 March	Saville Theatre, London
7 March	Winter Gardens, Malvern
9 March	The Marquee
10 March	UFO
11 March	Canterbury Technical College
12 March	The Agincourt, Camberley
15 March	EMI: 'Chapter 24'
16 March	EMI: 'Flaming'
17 March	Kingston Technical College
18 March	Enfield College
20 March	EMI, two sessions: 'Take Up Thy Stethoscope', 'The Scarecrow'
21 March	EMI, two sessions: 'Pow R Toc H'
22 March	EMI: mixing
23 March	Clifton Hall, Rotherham
24 March	The Ricky Tick, Hounslow
25 March	The Ricky Tick, Windsor
26 March	The Shoreline, Bognor Regis
28 March	Corn Exchange, Bristol

29 March	a) EMI: 'The Gnome'
	b) Eel Pie Island Hotel
31 March	Top Spot Ballroom, Ross-on-Wye
1 April	The Birdcage Dancehall, Portsmouth
3 April	BBC Playhouse Theatre, Northumberland Avenue, London
6 April	City Hall, Salisbury
7 April	Floral Hall, Belfast
8 April	a) Rhodes Centre, Bishops Stortford
	b) The Roundhouse
9 April	Britannia Rowing Club, Nottingham
10 April	Bath Pavilion, Bath
11 April	EMI: 'Astronomy Domine'
12 April	EMI, two sessions: mixing, 'Lucifer Sam'
13 April	a) The Railway Club, Tilbury
	b) EMI: 'Lucifer'
15 April	West Pier Ballroom, Brighton
17 April	EMI, two sessions: overdubbing, 'Astronomy'
18 April	EMI, two sessions: 'She Was a Millionaire', 'Lucifer', 'Astronomy'
19 April	The Bromley Court Hotel, Bromley
20 April	Queen's Hall, Barnstaple
21 April	a) The Starlite, Greenford
	b) UFO
22 April	Benn Memorial Hall, Rugby
23 April	Starlight Ballroom, Crawley
24 April	The Feathers, Ealing Broadway, London
25 April	The Stage Club, Oxford
28 April	The Tabernacle Club, Stockport
29 April	a) Zaandam, nr Amsterdam, Holland
	b) '14 Hour Technicolor Dream', Alexandra Palace, London

30 April	Plaza Teen Club, Huddersfield
3 May	The Moulin Rouge club, Ainsdale
4 May	The Locarno club, Coventry
5 May	UFO
6 May	Kitson College, Leeds
7 May	The King and Queen Mojo A Go-Go, Sheffield
12 May	a) 'Games for May', Queen Elizabeth Hall, South Bank, London b) EMI: 'Astronomy'
13 May	St George's Ballroom, Hinckley
19 May	Club A' Go Go, Newcastle
20 May	Floral Hall, Southport
21 May	a) EMI: 'Bike' b) Sound Techniques: 'See Emily Play'
23 May	Town Hall, High Wycombe
24 May	Bromley Court Hotel
25 May	Grosmont Wood Farm, Abergavenny
26 May	Empress Ballroom, Blackpool
27 May	Civic Hall, Nantwich
29 May	Tulip Bulb Auction Hall, Spalding
1 June	EMI: 'Bike', 'Lucifer'
2 June	UFO
5 June	EMI, two sessions: 'Chapter 24', 'Bike', 'Interstellar'
7 June	EMI: mixing
9 June	Hull College of Technology and Commerce
10 June	The Nautilus Club, Lowestoft
11 June	a) The Immage, Terneuzen, Holland b) Concertgebouw, Vlissingen, Holland
13 June	The Feathers
15 June	Free concert, Abbey Wood Park, Kent

16 June	The Tiles, Oxford
17 June	The Dreamland Ballroom, Margate
18 June	Brands Hatch, Kent
20 June	'Commem Ball', Magdalen College, Oxford
21 June	Bolton College Midsummer Ball, Rivington Barn, Horwich
22 June	Bradford University
23 June	The Locarno, Derby
24 June	Cesars Club, Bedford
25 June	Mister Smiths, Manchester (two shows)
26 June	Warwick University
27 June	EMI: overdubbing
28 June	Eel Pie Island Hotel
29 June	EMI: mixing
30 June	EMI: mixing
1 July	The Swan, Yardley
3 July	Bath Pavilion
5 July	a) Eel Pie Island Hotel b) EMI: recording links
8 July	Memorial Hall, Northwich
9 July	The Roundhouse
13 July	EMI: banding and cutting the mono LP *Piper at the Gates of Dawn*
15 July	The Cricket Meadow, Stowmarket Carnival
16 July	Redcar Jazz Club, Redcar
18 July	a) The Palace, Douglas, Isle of Man b) EMI, two sessions: stereo mixing
19 July	Floral Hall, Gorleston
20 July	Two Red Shoes Ballroom, Elgin
21 July	Ballerina Ballroom, Nairn
22 July	The Beach Ballroom, Aberdeen
23 July	Cosmopolitan Ballroom, Carlisle

24 July	The Maryland, Glasgow
25 July	Greenock Palladium, Greenock
28 July	a) BBC Playhouse Theatre b) UFO c) EMI: abandoned due to Barrett's behaviour
29 July	a) The Wellington Club, East Dereham b) 'Love In Festival', Alexandra Palace
31 July	Town Hall, Torquay
7 August	EMI: 'Scream Thy Last Scream'
8 August	EMI: 'Set the Controls for the Heart of the Sun'
15 August	Sound Techniques: 'Reaction in G', 'Untitled', both abandoned
16 August	Sound Techniques: 'Reaction', 'Untitled', again both abandoned
1 September	The Roundhouse
2 September	The Roundhouse
4 September	Sound Techniques: 'Untitled'
5 September	Sound Techniques: 'Untitled'
6 September	Sound Techniques: 'Untitled'
9 September	Boom Dancing Centre, Aarhus, Denmark
10 September	Gyllene Cirkeln, Stockholm, Sweden
11 September	Starclub, Copenhagen, Denmark
12 September	Starclub
13 September	Starclub
15 September	The Starlite, Belfast
16 September	The Flamingo, Ballymena
17 September	The Arcadia, Cork
19 September	The Speakeasy, Margaret Street, London
21 September	Assembly Hall, Worthing
22 September	The Tiles, Oxford
23 September	The Corn Exchange, Chelmsford

25 September	BBC Playhouse Theatre
27 September	The Fifth Dimension, Leicester
28 September	The Skyline Ballroom, Hull
30 September	The Imperial, Nelson
1 October	Saville Theatre, London
6 October	Top Rank Suite, Brighton
7 October	Victoria Rooms, Bristol
9 October	Recording at De Lane Lea Studios, Kingsway, London: 'Remember A Day', 'Jugband Blues', 'Vegetable Man'
11 October	De Lane Lea Studios: 'Remember', 'Jugband', 'Vegetable'
12 October	De Lane Lea Studios: 'Remember', 'Vegetable'
13 October	The Pavilion, Weymouth
14 October	Cesars Club, Bedford
16 October	Bath Pavilion
19 October	De Lane Lea Studios: 'Jugband'
20 October	De Lane Lea Studios: unknown work
21 October	York University
23 October	De Lane Lea Studios, two sessions: 'Untitled', 'Set the Controls', 'Early Morning Henry'
24 October	De Lane Lea Studios: 'Untitled'
26 October	De Lane Lea Studios: 'Untitled', 'Apples and Oranges'
27 October	De Lane Lea Studios: 'Apples'
28 October	Durham University
2 November	The Fillmore Auditorium, San Francisco
3 November	The Winterland Auditorium, San Francisco
5 November	The Cheetah Club, Santa Monica
9 November	The Fillmore
10 November	The Winterland
11 November	The Winterland

12 November	The Cheetah, New York
13 November	Ahoy Hallen, Rotterdam, Holland
14 November	a) Royal Albert Hall b) EMI: 'Apples', 'Paintbox'
15 November	Winter Gardens, Bournemouth (two shows)
17 November	City Hall, Sheffield (two shows)
18 November	Empire Theatre, Liverpool (two shows)
19 November	Coventry Theatre, Coventry (two shows)
22 November	The Guildhall, Portsmouth (two shows)
23 November	Sophia Gardens, Cardiff (two shows)
24 November	Colston Hall, Bristol (two shows)
25 November	The Opera House, Blackpool (two shows)
26 November	Palace Theatre, Manchester (two shows)
27 November	Queens College, Belfast (two shows)
1 December	Central Hall, Chatham (two shows)
2 December	The Dome, Brighton (two shows)
3 December	Theatre Royal, Nottingham (two shows)
4 December	City Hall, Newcastle (two shows)
5 December	Green's Playhouse, Glasgow (two shows)
6 December	Royal College of Art, Kensington, London
8 December	Chislehurst Caves, Chislehurst
13 December	The Flamingo Club, Redruth
14 December	The Pavilion, Bournemouth
15 December	The Middle Earth, Covent Garden, London
16 December	a) The Ritz Ballroom, Birmingham b) The Penthouse, Birmingham
20 December	a) Recording at BBC Studios, Maida Vale, London: 'Vegetable', 'Scream', 'Jugband', 'Pow R Toc H' b) EMI: 'Scream'
21 December	The Speakeasy
22 December	Olympia Exhibition Hall, London

1968

10 January	EMI: 'Untitled'
11 January	EMI: 'Set the Controls for the Heart of the Sun', 'Scream'
12 January	Aston University, Birmingham
13 January	Winter Gardens Pavilion, Weston-Super-Mare
19 January	Town Hall, Lewes
20 January	Hastings Pier, Hastings
24 January	EMI: rehearsal
30 January	Sound Techniques: abandoned
6 May	a) CBS Recording Studios, Theobalds Road, London: tape-to-tape transfers b) EMI: 'Silas Lang', 'Swan Lee', 'Late Night'
14 May	EMI: 'Rhamadan', 'Lanky', 'Golden Hair'
21 May	EMI: 'Silas', 'Late Night'
28 May	EMI, two sessions: 'Swan', 'Golden', 'Rhamadan'
8 June	EMI: 'Swan'
20 June	EMI: 'Swan', 'Late', 'Golden'
27 June	EMI: 'Swan', 'Late', 'Golden'
20 July	EMI: 'Swan', 'Late', 'Golden', 'Octopus'

1969

No concert appearances

10 April	EMI: 'Swan', 'Octopus'
11 April	EMI: 'Opel', 'Love You', 'It's No Good Trying', 'Terrapin', 'Late', 'Golden'
17 April	EMI: 'No Man's Land', 'Here I Go'
23 April	EMI: 'Rhamadan'

25 April	EMI: 'No Good', 'Terrapin', 'Octopus', 'Love You', 'Golden', 'Late', 'Swan', 'Love You'
3 May	EMI: 'Love You', 'No Good', 'Octopus'
4 May	EMI: 'No Good', 'Terrapin', 'No Man's'
6 May	EMI: 'No Good', 'Opel', 'Golden', 'Late', 'Swan', 'No Man's', 'Here I Go', 'Rhamadan'
12 June	EMI: 'Octopus', 'Golden', 'Dark Globe', 'Long Gone'
13 June	EMI: 'Octopus'
26 July	EMI: 'She Took a Long Cold Look', 'Long Gone', 'Globe', 'Feel', 'If It's In You'
5 August	EMI, two sessions: mixing
16 September	EMI: mixing
6 October	EMI: editing
9 October	EMI: banding the stereo-only LP *The Madcap Laughs*
17 December	EMI: 'Religious Experience' for Kevin Ayers
18 December	EMI: mixing

1970

12 January	EMI: mixing
24 February	BBC Studios: 'Gigolo Aunt', 'Terrapin', 'Baby Lemonade', 'Effervescing Elephant', 'Two of a Kind'
26 February	BBC Studios: 'Lemonade', 'Maisie'
27 February	EMI: 'Wolfpack', 'Waving My Arms', 'Living Alone', 'Bob Dylan Blues', 'Gigolo'
1 April	EMI: 'Gigolo', 'Lemonade'
2 April	EMI: 'Lemonade', 'Waving'

3 April	EMI: 'Waving', 'Wolfpack', 'Gigolo', 'Lemonade', 'Maisie'
6 June	Olympia Exhibition Hall
7 June	EMI, two sessions: 'Milky Way', 'Millionaire', 'Birdie Hop', 'Rats', 'Wined and Dined'
14 July	EMI, two sessions: 'Wined', 'Elephant', 'Dolly Rocker', 'Love Song', 'Let's Split', 'Dominoes'
15 July	EMI, two sessions: 'Dominoes'
17 July	EMI, two sessions: 'Elephant', 'Love Song'
21 July	EMI: 'Word Song', 'It Is Obvious'
22 July	EMI, three sessions: 'Obvious', 'Gigolo', 'Waving', 'Wolfpack', 'Elephant'
23 July	EMI, three sessions: 'Wined', 'Obvious', 'Rats', 'Dominoes', 'Lemonade', mixing
24 July	EMI, two sessions: mixing and banding the LP *Barrett*
1 September	EMI: remixing

1971

No concert appearances

16 February	BBC Studios, Shepherd's Bush, London

1972

No recording sessions

Early	King's College Cellar, Cambridge
Early	Corn Exchange, Cambridge
Early	Dandelion café, Cambridge
Early	Market Square, Cambridge
24 February	Corn Exchange

ACKNOWLEDGEMENTS AND SOURCES

For further reading, consult *Lost in the Woods* by Julian Palacios (Boxtree) and *Crazy Diamond* by Mike Watkinson and Pete Anderson (Omnibus). But beware. The former is confusingly written and contains some elementary errors; the latter is desperately inaccurate. Both, however, do include interviews with some of Barrett's intimates, and Palacios' book contains a wealth of primary sources in its footnotes, including a seminal essay by Nick Kent. Obsessive Barrettomanes may also wish to peruse *Random Precision: Recording the Music of Syd Barrett, 1965-1974* by David Parker (Cherry Red Books). Though he is (almost) accurate to the last detail, Parker rarely strays beyond the confines of the studio, thus making his account about as gripping to the general reader as a tram timetable.

Thanks to the following for talking to me: Peter Barnes, Alan Barrett, Roger Barrett, Viv Brans, Abigail Chisman, Lindsay Corner, Marc Dessier, Duggie Fields, Jock Findlay, David Gale, Libby Gausden, David Gilmour, Kari-Ann Jagger, Sue Kingsford, Rado 'Bob' Klose, Jenny Lesmoir-Gordon, Gala Pinion, Aubrey 'Po' Powell, Andrew Rawlinson, Mick Rock, Anthony Stern, Storm Thorgerson, Mary and Roger Waters, Mary Wing, Juliet Wright, Emily Young, and all those who prefer to remain anonymous. Thanks also to Jon Old, for a brilliant idea; to Dion Johnson, Colin Turner and Philip Waters for their assistance; to Anna Muggeridge for her sub-editing skills; and to Polly Samson for her unfailing help and support. Eternal gratitude to Polly's husband David Gilmour, without whom etc. Apologies to David Bowie for picking on him when so many others are also guilty. Love and thanks to Joanna and Imogen, who have had to endure some pretty mad behaviour themselves.

LDS

G000143836

JOURNEYS INTO HERTFORDSHIRE

The collection of nearly 200 ink drawings depicts the buildings and landscape of the still predominantly rural county of Hertfordshire. After four years of searching, the author presents his personal choice of memorable images, capturing the delights of a hitherto relatively unfêted part of England.

The area is rich in subtle contrasts – from the steep, wooded slopes of the Chilterns to the wide-open spaces of the north-east and the urban fringes of London in the south. Ancient market towns, an impressive cathedral city and countless small villages are surrounded by an intimate landscape of rolling farmland.

The drawings range widely over all manner of dwellings from stately home to simple cottage and over ecclesiastical buildings from cathedral to parish church. They portray bridges, mills and farmsteads, chalk downs and watery river valleys, busy street scenes and secluded village byways.

The accompanying notes are deliberately concise but serve to entice readers to make their own journeys around this charming county.

'Anthony Mackay's pen-and-ink drawings are of outstanding quality. An architectural graduate, he is equally at home depicting landscapes and buildings. The medium he uses is, in a master's hands, better able to show both depth and detail than any photograph and I have rarely seen the equal of the drawings that grace this book.'

Bedfordshire Life

Anthony Mackay

The author and artist was born in Cheshire in 1937, and developed an early affection for rural landscape, and an interest in drawing.

Since graduating in architecture from the University of Liverpool in 1961, he has designed buildings in Denmark, Greece, the Middle East, Germany and Britain, and practises in Bedford.

His extensive travels in Europe, the United States and India have resulted in paintings, pastels and ink drawings, many of which have been exhibited publicly and been bought for private collections.

His first book 'Journeys into Bedfordshire' was published in 1987, the most recent, Journeys into Buckinghamshire in 1998.

JOURNEYS INTO HERTFORDSHIRE

A COLLECTION OF
INK DRAWINGS

ANTHONY MACKAY

FOREWORD BY

THE MARQUESS OF SALISBURY

This pocket edition first published November 2001

Original edition first published October 1991 by
The Book Castle
12 Church Street
Dunstable
Bedfordshire LU5 4RU

ISBN 1 903747 10 4

Printed by Interprint Ltd., Malta.

Front Cover: St Albans Cathedral
Back Cover: Hatfield House

HATFIELD PARK OAK

CONTENTS

To
Hortensia Constance
and
Alida Wilhelmina

FOREWORD
by
THE MARQUESS OF SALISBURY

HATFIELD HOUSE,
HATFIELD,
HERTFORDSHIRE.

I have much pleasure in writing the Foreword to Anthony Mackay's intriguing collection of ink drawings which have been splendidly presented in this volume. They represent a fine record of the buildings and landscape of Hertfordshire.

It is the result of four years of researches and sketching, and ranges over a spectrum of architecture from stately homes to humble cottages, and it shows clearly that, despite proximity to London and its pressures, our county remains essentially rural in character. It demonstrates that it is possible to conserve and rejuvenate the old whilst coping with the need for change and development.

The drawings reveal great diversity in building styles and construction for such a small county, and reflect the enormous impact which trees, water and open space have upon the environment.

The book will encourage others to go out and explore Hertfordshire for themselves, and to discover hidden depths in its history and culture.

Salisbury

Marquess of Salisbury

ACKNOWLEDGEMENTS

For permission to make drawings and to use them in this volume, I would like to thank the following individuals and institutions, who kindly allowed me onto their land and gave me invaluable help in compiling information about their buildings.

Ashridge Management College
The Trustees of the Abel Smith 1964 Settlement, Woodhall Park
Baroness Birk of Rentstreet Barns, Bovingdon
Mr Simon Bowes Lyon of St Paul's Walden Bury
Mrs Jean Broadribb of Whitehall Farmhouse, Luffenhall
Mr and Mrs Butler of Standon Lordship
Mr R. Brandling, Headteacher of Dewhurst St Mary JMI School, Cheshunt
Mr and Mrs Godfrey Cockerton of Elm Cottage, Hare Street
Miss Davies of Pirton Grange
Mr Andrew Graham-Stewart of Little Gaddesden Manor
Mr and Mrs J. Herbert of The Hall, Much Hadham
Hertfordshire County Council
Hertford Museum
Miss E. A. Kennedy and Mr L. J. Kitto of Wallington
Mr David Laing of Mackerye End, Harpenden
Mr R. Latchford of Cromer Farm
The Marquess and Marchioness of Salisbury of Hatfield House
Mr A. J. and Mrs A. T. Mead
Mr John Mills of Hinxworth Place
Moor Park Golf Club
The National Trust
Mr Norman Swallow of Fabdens Park, Cold Christmas
and many others who have unwittingly contributed.

In addition I would like to thank Mr Robin Harcourt-Williams MA, Librarian and Archivist to the Marquess of Salisbury, for his valuable assistance.

To Miss Dorothy Abel Smith, who diligently checked and corrected my manuscript for style and historical accuracy, and who extended my knowledge of the county, I owe a special debt of gratitude.

Finally I thank Mrs R. I. White for typing the text, and my wife Elaine for the patience and support she has shown over the four years during which the book was prepared.

THE HORNS, BULL'S GREEN

HATFIELD HOUSE

INTRODUCTION

Hertfordshire is a land of subtle contrasts. From the steep wooded escarpments of the Chilterns to the wide open spaces of the north east flank, ancient market towns, an impressive cathedral city, and countless small villages, nestle in an intimate landscape of rolling farmland. The encroaching urban tentacles of London have brought formless sprawl to the southern fringes, and here much of the historic fabric has been blurred, but despite this and the ravages of major roads and railways serving the capital, the overwhelming character of the county is deeply rural, in which the fine grain of old communities and the evolutionary patterns of agriculture have left enduring marks. Grand gesture is absent, but close study unearths a rich seam of natural landscape and vernacular architecture.

The former Roman city of Verulamium has all but vanished, but was the forerunner of St Albans, with its magnificent cathedral dwarfing the narrow medieval streets and market place and towering over the valley of the River Ver below. Old market towns such as Hertford, Bishop's Stortford and Royston have retained their original street patterns, and their many elegant buildings reflect cultured societies with an acute awareness of good craftsmanship and design. Much Hadham, Ashwell, Benington and Barkway are classic English villages, and throughout the county stately homes and humble cottages chart centuries of enlightened building. Proximity to London, The Royal Court and Parliament led to several important country mansions, the most celebrated of which is at Hatfield, where the earlier Tudor palace was succeeded by one of England's finest Jacobean houses.

Myriad streams course down through the Hertfordshire countryside forming wetlands and rivers which eventually drain into the Thames at the heart of the London docklands. Neolithic settlement of the county took place from the fourth or third millennia BC, and round barrows along the Icknield Way belong to the

Bronze Age, but there is a distinct lack of important sites. A major Iron Age fort was constructed at Ravensburgh Castle, near Hexton, and several items of pottery have been unearthed which, together with other finds at Willian and Holwell, confirm the concentration of human activity on the Chilterns.

In pre-Roman times the county was partially occupied by the Catuvellauni tribe, whose capital was originally at Wheathampstead, evidence of which can be seen today in the ditches of Devil's Dyke, but which was moved to St Albans under Tasciovanus in 15BC and based in Prae Wood, where a substantial township developed. After the Roman invasion in 43AD the Catuvellauni were quickly defeated, and the Verulamium military settlement was established. At Gorhambury, St Albans, and at Gadebridge, Hemel Hempstead, examples of Roman villas from the first century AD have been excavated. The lack of Saxon placenames in Hertfordshire suggests that the Romano-British population may have withstood the influx of settlers in the centuries after the Roman occupation.

The buildings of the county have naturally been influenced from early times by the available local materials. Chalk was once much used as a building stone and flint was also common, but timber provided the structure for most housing and for the roofs of major buildings. In the eastern part of Hertfordshire many buildings are enriched by pargetting, plaster work with patterns and ornamentation incised with a wooden comb or stick but occasionally formed in relief using moulds. Weatherboarding for cottages and farm buildings was common, and survives in many places, but the use of thatch, which was the usual roofing material for timber-framed buildings, has almost died out and been replaced by tiles. The clays which overlay the chalk strata produced the bricks and tiles which have dominated building since Tudor times. Hatfield House and Mackerye End are superb examples of early brick architecture, and the character of most Hertfordshire towns is based on brick.

Elizabethan and Jacobean houses are plentiful and of high

METHODIST CHAPEL, BALDOCK

quality, and include Queen Hoo, near Tewin, Water End, Wheathampstead, the Manor House, Barkway, Delamere House, Great Wymondley, and Upp Hall, Braughing.

Of the surviving timber hall houses Clintons at Little Hadham, Walnut Tree Farm at Luffenhall and Place House at Ware are largely intact, as are timber-framed barns at Croxley Green.

There are many fine 17th century houses, foremost amongst which are Balls Park, Tyttenhanger, Romeland House, St Albans, Brent Pelham Hall and The Hall, Much Hadham. Important remnants of Wren's work can be found at Tring Park and in the Temple Bar which was moved to Theobalds Park in the 19th century. At Ashridge, Little Gaddesden, one of the country's most spectacular neo-gothic mansions was completed by Wyatville, with parkland by Capability Brown and Repton, whose work can also be seen at Moor Park, Wrotham Park, Brookmans, Cassiobury, Panshanger and Tewin Water. Other great 18th century houses which survive are Brocket, Woodhall, Gorhambury and Wormleybury.

Breweries and maltings, watermills and windmills record the industrial heritage of the county. The Grand Union and New River canals bring the fascinating architecture of locks and bridges, and the colour of brightly painted barges to the landscape. Ecclesiastical buildings dominate every kind of settlement and reflect the peak of artistic achievement amongst the modest communities of this understated but charming segment of middle England.

The drawings were made between 1986 and 1991 and represent a personal and often idiosyncratic choice of subject, providing neither a comprehensive guide nor by any means a complete record. Even at this stage it seems that only the surface of the county has been scratched and that so much of interest has had to be omitted.

Anthony Mackay
Bedford 1991

UP FISHPOOL STREET, ST ALBANS

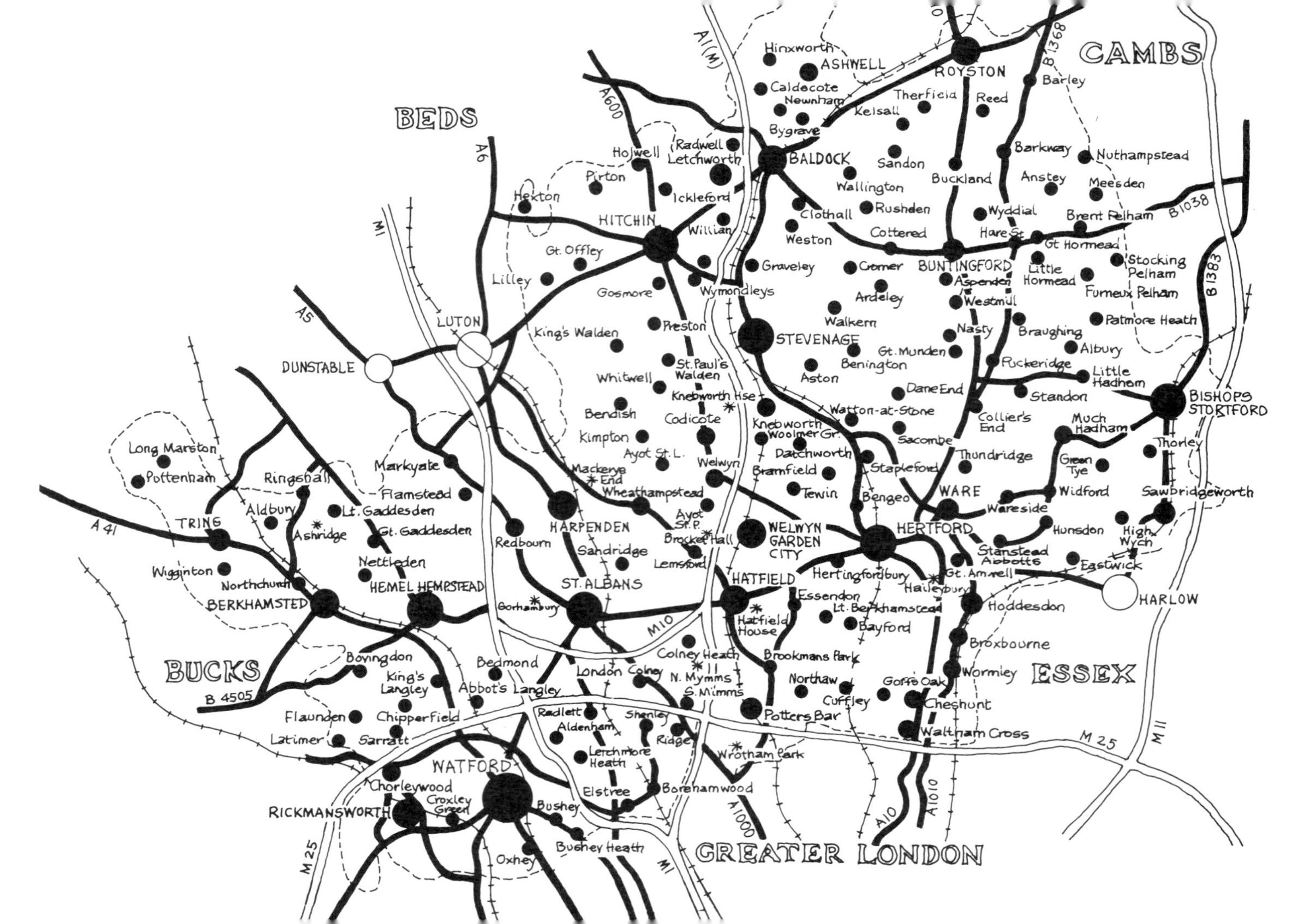
CAMBS
BEDS
BUCKS
ESSEX
GREATER LONDON
Hinxworth
ASHWELL
ROYSTON
Barley
Caldecote
Newnham
Therfield
Reed
Kelsall
Bygrave
Radwell
Holwell
Letchworth
BALDOCK
Sandon
Barkway
Nuthampstead
Pirton
Wallington
Buckland
Anstey
Meesden
Hexton
Ickleford
Clothall
Rushden
Wyddial
Brent Pelham
HITCHIN
William
Weston
Cottered
Hare St
Gt Hormead
BUNTINGFORD
Gt. Offley
Graveley
Cromer
Little Hormead
Stocking Pelham
Lilley
Gosmore
Wymondleys
Ardeley
Aspenden
Westmill
Furneux Pelham
LUTON
Walkern
Braughing
Patmore Heath
King's Walden
Preston
STEVENAGE
Nasty
Albury
DUNSTABLE
Gt. Munden
St. Paul's Walden
Benington
Puckeridge
Little Hadham
Whitwell
Aston
Dane End
Standon
BISHOPS STORTFORD
Knebworth Hse
Bendish
Codicote
Knebworth
Watton-at-Stone
Collier's End
Much Hadham
Kimpton
Woolmer Gr.
Sacombe
Thorley
Long Marston
Ayot St. L.
Datchworth
Thundridge
Green Tye
Pottenham
Ringshall
Markyate
Mackerye End
Welwyn
Bramfield
Stapleford
Flamstead
Wheathampstead
Tewin
Bengeo
WARE
Widford
Sawbridgeworth
Aldbury
Lt. Gaddesden
Wareside
TRING
Ashridge
Gt. Gaddesden
Redbourn
HARPENDEN
Ayot St. P.
Brocket Hall
WELWYN GARDEN CITY
HERTFORD
Hunsdon
High Wych
Sandridge
Stanstead Abbotts
Nettleden
Lemsford
Hertingfordbury
Gt. Amwell
Eastwick
Wigginton
Northchurch
HEMEL HEMPSTEAD
ST. ALBANS
HATFIELD
Haileybury
HARLOW
BERKHAMSTED
Gorhambury
Essendon
Hoddesdon
Hatfield House
Lt. Berkhamstead
Bayford
Colney Heath
Broxbourne
Bovingdon
Bedmond
Brookmans Park
King's Langley
London Colney
N. Mymms
Northaw
Goffs Oak
Wormley
Abbot's Langley
S. Mimms
Cuffley
Cheshunt
Flaunden
Chipperfield
Radlett
Shenley
Potters Bar
Aldenham
Ridge
Waltham Cross
Latimer
Sarratt
Letchmore Heath
Wrotham Park
WATFORD
Chorleywood
Elstree
Borehamwood
Croxley Green
RICKMANSWORTH
Bushey
Bushey Heath
Oxhey
A1(M)
A600
A6
A5
M1
A41
B4505
M10
M25
A1000
A10
A1010
M11
B1368
B1038
B1383

ASHWELL, ROYSTON AND THE NORTH

As the countryside opens out towards the plains of East Anglia the fields become larger, the woodlands more sparse and the skies more expansive in this underpopulated corner of the county.

In early medieval times the unfortunate effects of animal disease and repeated spells of bad weather caused severe depopulation and even the abandonment of many settlements, and subsequent plagues in the late 14th century further reduced the population. Despite these problems there are some beautifully composed surviving villages, and the remarkable churches at Ashwell and Anstey amongst others reflect clearly the unquenchable artistic and religious spirit of those troubled times. Barkway, Brent Pelham and Royston have retained their distinctive medieval structure and character in spite of recent growth. Pre-Roman Icknield Way and Roman Ermine Street intersect at Royston, around which junction elegant 17th and 18th century houses and inns were built to cope with a thriving coaching trade.

Building materials were traditionally local and there are many good examples of timber-framed, thatched and weatherboarded dwellings and farmhouses, and later brick and clay-tile houses, when forest in the area gave way to farmland and man was increasingly constrained to extract building materials from the earth. Churches, as the most important and prominent buildings, are generally constructed of soft chalk or limestone quarried in Hertfordshire or at Totternhoe in Bedfordshire, and often combined with flint in chequered patterns to give enduring structural

ASHWELL MUSEUM

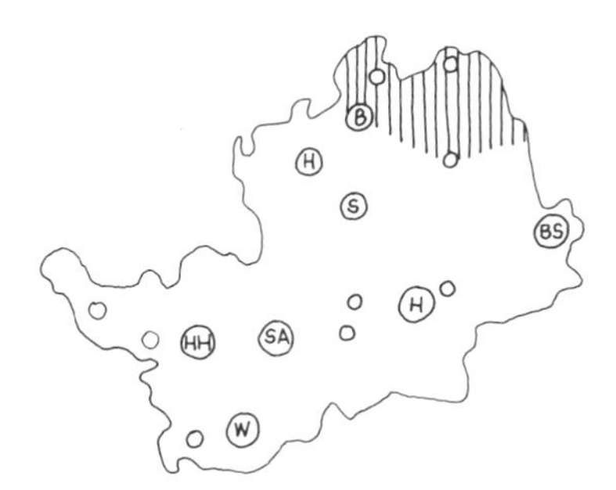

stability. The church towers of Ashwell and Anstey are distinguished by sheathed wooden Hertfordshire spikes. During the 19th century yellow bricks came into use in the area, the added lime modifying the normal reddish iron colour present in local clays. This area has remained least affected by urban development and has a somewhat forgotten and neglected air despite its proximity to motorways and to the metropolis.

KING'S LODGE, ROYSTON

FORESTERS COTTAGES, ASHWELL

ASHWELL

Ashwell is dominated by St Mary's Church with its 176 foot high tower topped by octagonal lantern and spike, a perfect symbol of the importance of this former market town. Clustered compactly around the church and in the High Street are many well preserved houses dating from the 15th century onwards, disporting timber framing, brickwork and plastered construction in a delightful minor symphony of traditional architecture.

A tiny museum is housed in the 500 year old Town House. The Guildhall of St John the Baptist is dated 1476 and neighbouring cottages with fancy pargetting were built in 1681. Forrester's cottages were completely restored in 1962-63 and together with Ashwell Bury, 16th century Ducklake farmhouse with Tudor wall paintings, and the Georgian rectory, underline the substantial architectural qualities of this charming place.

◁ *MILL STREET, ASHWELL*

FORMER BUTCHER'S SHOP, ASHWELL

HINXWORTH PLACE

HINXWORTH: CALDECOTE: NEWNHAM

Hinxworth Place, which is situated outside the village of *Hinxworth*, is one of the best preserved 15th to 16th century stone manor houses in Hertfordshire, and was once inhabited by Cistercian monks.

The church of St Nicholas stands alone at the edge of the village. Timber-framed thatched cottages are scattered throughout the village, prominent amongst which is Middle Farm, a long, low building.

The disused church of St Mary Magdalene at *Caldecote* stands forlornly in an overgrown farm yard. In the porch a unique canopied and crocketed holy water stoup gathers green mould, and the octagonal font has traceried and cusped panels with foliage under the bowl.

The outwardly dull church of St Vincent in *Newnham* has some stunning medieval wall paintings depicting St Christopher paddling across a stream filled with fish.

◁ *ST MARY'S CHURCH TOWER, ASHWELL*

HINXWORTH CHURCH

HIGH STREET, ROYSTON

ROYSTON

Tucked against the Cambridgeshire border, the ancient market town of *Royston* is on the crossing of the Icknield Way and Roman Ermine Street, and has some intriguing features, prominent amongst which is the Royston Cave, a bottle shaped cavern containing carved reliefs of the crucifixion of St Christopher, and of several kings and queens, all of uncertain date and origin (discovered in 1742). Roysia's Stone lies at the crossing and is reputed to be the base of an ancient cross. King James I's hunting lodge in Kneesworth Street, which was known as the Palace, has survived in part as a range with massive chimneys and a shell-hooded door between, and it was from here that the king hunted on Royston Common.

The parish church of St John and St Thomas is part of the church of the 12th century monastery of Augustinian Canons which existed at the crossroads, and is an amalgam of fragments dating from this time up to a major restoration in 1872. In the High Street the Chequers Hotel (15th century) has a jettied front, and many houses built during the 18th century have fine classical details. Other notable buildings are the Court House (1849) in John Street, The Priory, and the former Corn Exchange (1830) which had an internal courtyard with a colonnade of fluted cast iron columns. Upper King Street has several rambling, overhung and plastered houses, many of which are being restored.

Royston Museum is housed in a converted Congregational chapel opposite the Palace, and has an interesting collection of historical photographs and paintings of the town.

SANDON: THERFIELD: KELSHALL

The church, a 16th century cottage and the Six Bells Inn cluster around the hilltop at the centre of *Sandon*, and the land slopes away to the west exposing long rural views over the North Hertfordshire countryside.

At Sandon Mount nearby, the earthworks of England's oldest known windmill are obscured now by trees, but are fascinating historical remains.

In *Therfield* a narrow lane flanked by thatched and overhung cottages leads from the green to the church, which was totally restored in 1878 incorporating fragments of its medieval predecessor. The focus of the village is a small green surrounded by cottages, mature trees and gardens. The old Rectory was probably the manor house and has 15th to 18th century elements. Stone mullions, cusps and mouldings appear in the windows. Nearby Tuthill Manor was converted from a derelict timber-framed farmhouse dated 1480 into an attractive house. Therfield Heath has five burial mounds and a long barrow, and is the home of rare flora such as the pasque flower and burnt-tip orchid.

Kelsall's much restored church of St Faith is approached along a leafy lane and stands enclosed by mature trees in its walled churchyard next to the late Georgian Rectory. The village lies on an exposed chalk ridge overlooking the Bedfordshire/Cambridgeshire plain to the north and in a land of plunging fields and well defined coppices.

ALL SAINTS CHURCH, SANDON

LANDSCAPE NEAR THERFIELD

KELSALL CHURCH

WALLINGTON

NUTSHAMPSTEAD: WALLINGTON: REED: BYGRAVE: THROCKING

A memorial to the 378th Heavy Bombardment Group USAF was erected in 1983 outside the Woodman Inn at Nuthampstead in tribute to the troops using the runway laid here during the Second World War. The runway has now disappeared and Nuthampstead has reverted to an obscure agricultural hamlet with its weather-boarded and thatched cottages.

At the centre of *Wallington* stands a minute cottage, a thatched and pargetted dwelling common in these parts, but made special because George Orwell, the novelist and essayist, lived here from 1936 to 1940 and wrote the classic work 'The Road to Wigan Pier' whilst simultaneously running the small shop. He and his wife raised hens and goats and lived the simple country life here, bicycling or walking along narrow lanes to Letchworth and Walkern to attend meetings or visit friends in those unsettling days leading to the outbreak of war. Rectory and Bury stand together on high ground amongst the trees. St Mary's is wholly perpendicular and has a fine south porch, a spacious nave, and gnarled oak pews.

Reed is dispersed around three greens, one of which, Fiddler's Green, has a pub and cricket pitch, and a small Victorian school. St Mary's church has traces of late Anglo-Saxon work in the nave and Reed Hall stands in moated grounds.

Bygrave is notable for its ancient earthworks, and for the Norman nave and doorway of St Margaret's Church. Long views over three counties can be enjoyed from the hilltop.

In the late Middle Ages *Throcking* was deserted, but the church has an interesting 13th century west tower of flint and brick, with a corbelled-out stair turret and a parapet built in 1660. Poppyhead ends to the choir stalls depict acrobats.

CHURCH LANE, BARKWAY

BARKWAY: BARLEY

One of the unspoilt gems of Hertfordshire, *Barkway* has a magnificent long High Street lined with well-kept buildings, which reflect its former importance as a coaching town. At the north end a late 14th century hall house with jettied gable stands end on to the street. The Red House is early Georgian with an elegant doorcase displaying fluted pilasters and a triglyph frieze. The High Street is without street lighting and the absence of lamp standards contributes greatly to its unspoilt quality.

Set in an open landscape of vast prairie-like fields on the chalky Cambridgeshire border, *Barley* was a home for Archbishops of Canterbury, professors at Cambridge University, and the first mayor of New York, Mr Thomas Willett. Homestalls is a Tudor building with 1913 additions by the architect Barry Parker of Letchworth Garden City fame, and is tile-hung, herring-boned and rought-cast. The rainwater pipes are decorated with vine leaves. Dalny Veed (1907) also belongs firmly to the Arts and Crafts movement. The Fox and Hounds Inn sign depicting huntsmen and fox, spans the road on a long beam at the entrance to the village from Barkway.

Town House in Church End Lane dated 1526 served as school almshouses and was completely restored between 1969 and 1972 for use as the village hall. St Margaret's church was heavily restored by William Butterfield in 1871-2 and is a dull transformation of what was a fine perpendicular building.

At Cross Hill a 17th century timber framed lock-up cage reminds us of how drunkards were once treated in the village.

◁ *NUTHAMPSTEAD*

WEALDEN COTTAGES, BARKWAY

WEATHERBOARDING, BARKWAY

◁ *COTTAGES AT BARKWAY*

CHURCH END, BARLEY

FOX AND HOUNDS INN, BARLEY

OAK COTTAGE, HARE STREET

BUCKLAND: ANSTEY: HARE STREET

A missing stained glass inscription in *Buckland* church recorded a construction date of 1348. The south aisle arcade has pretty piers with capitals facing the aisle only.

Moated Buckland House is an elegant early Georgian house in chequered brickwork with a central doorcase with attached Ionic columns, and a Venetian window.

A square chequered brick dovecote can be seen at Pope's Hall in nearby Chipping.

Behind the unrestored and delightful church of St George in *Anstey* are the earthworks of a Norman castle, the motte partly filled with water. The bailey lies in the grounds of Anstey Hall.

The church tower is late Norman and the chancel is a superb example of Early English workmanship. The contemporary font is decorated with four twin-tailed mermen. Other interesting features include heraldic graffiti near the west arch of the tower, and a splendid 15th century lych gate, part of which was a 19th century lock-up.

Hare Street is scattered about the main road crossing two miles east of Buntingford. Houses of the 16th and 17th centuries with overhangs, such as the former Swan Inn, are complimented by Hare Street House, a Georgian red brick house with a small chapel sited in the grounds.

ANSTEY CHURCH

THE PELHAMS, THE HADHAMS AND BISHOPS STORTFORD

To the east of Roman Ermine Street and based on clays, sands and pebbles, the land slopes to the south where the streams of the Stort, the Ash and the Rib drain into the River Lea at Ware and Hertford.

Bishops Stortford is the principal market town and stands hard over on the Essex border. Down the spine of this area is a meandering road linking the Pelhams to the Hadhams and eventually connecting to Stanstead Abbots. To either side and buried in sumptuous countryside are countless greens and associated farmsteads of great rural charm.

Brent Pelham, Stocking Pelham and Furneux Pelham together with Little and Much Hadham are amongst the most beautiful villages of England, with their elegant country houses and clusters of picturesque cottages. All five have distinctly different plan shapes, varying from a scattering of buildings around a loose junction of lanes, to the assertive linear High Street of Much Hadham.

Tucked into the south eastern corner of the area is the maltings town of Sawbridgeworth with its weatherboarded mills, backing onto the River Stort, and handsome pargetted and brick town houses lining the main streets.

MUCH HADHAM

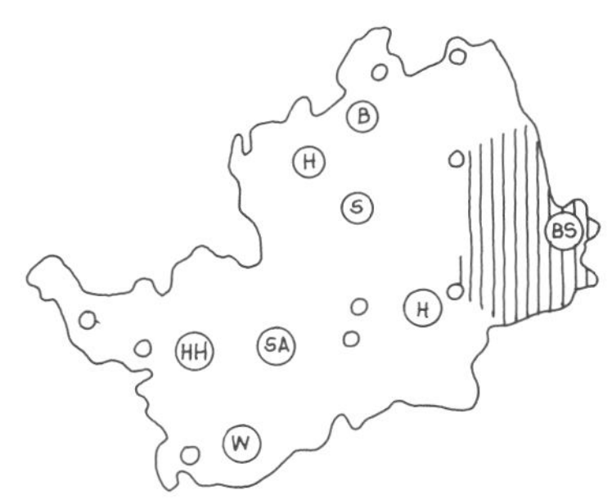

BRENT PELHAM: FURNEUX PELHAM: STOCKING PELHAM

At the heart of *Brent Pelham* the group of buildings comprising the church and a small terrace of thatched cottages is picturesque, but inside, the church is disappointing owing to insensitive restoration work. The black stone tomb of the local dragon-slayer, Piers Shonks, dates from the 13th century.

Furneux Pelham has several thatched half-timbered cottages and farm buildings, and focusses upon the large Perpendicular church of St Mary with its two-storeyed porch, tall unbuttressed tower with spike, stained glass by Morris and Burne-Jones, and a particularly fine tomb chest with brass figures, probably depicting Robert Newport and his wife, and dating from the early 15th century.

Furneux Pelham Hall is a 16th century manor house with stepped gables surrounded by beautiful gardens with old yew hedges, lawns, lakes and ornamental bridges.

Stocking Pelham is a tiny village of scattered farmsteads buried amongst hedged lanes, and has a small church with a fine double-ogee nave window.

WILLOW FARM COTTAGE, FURNEUX PELHAM

FURNEUX PELHAM COTTAGES ▷

BRENT PELHAM

THATCHED COTTAGE, FURNEUX PELHAM ▷

THE COCK INN, STOCKING PELHAM

GREAT HORMEAD

GREAT HORMEAD

Great Hormead has a very attractive village street with a mixture of thatched plastered cottages, weatherboarded barns and the 16th century Old Rectory. The church lies away from the main street behind Great Hormead Bury, and further to the north east, Brick House, a small early 16th century manor with stepped gables and brick mullioned windows, stands alone amongst tall trees at the end of a lane.

LITTLE HADHAM: MUCH HADHAM

Built where Stane Street crosses the River Ash, *Little Hadham* is clearly divided into three sections; at Hadham Ford where two 17th century houses overlook a small green and war memorial; at Church End where the church surveys the valley to the west and the once grand Hadham Hall, built partly in 1575, lies solidly at the end of its avenue; and at the crossroads where houses built between 1672 and 1732 cluster around the bottleneck and bridge.

The church of St Cecilia has a beautiful late medieval south porch built in timber with trefoiled open panels, and low box pews sit before a three-decked pulpit dated 1633.

The Bishops of London established a palace in *Much Hadham* in the 10th century. The present palace was built in the 16th century and refaced in the 17th century, and stands to the north of the churchyard. Edmund Tudor, the father of Henry VII was born here in 1430.

The village is emphatically one of the most beautiful in Hertfordshire, and is distinguished by the architectural quality and variety of its buildings. At the north end of the mile long High Street stands The Lordship (1740-45), a nine-bay, two-storey house with elegant stable block surmounted by a clock cupola. There is evidence of a substantial Tudor mansion having preceded the present house.

The church of St Andrew nestles amongst the trees and is set back from the High Street close to the River Ash. The west door of the tower has two head stops carved in 1953 by Henry Moore the sculptor, who lived nearby.

The Hall is a five-bay house with central Venetian window built between 1726 and 1729 reputedly by Nicholas Hawksmoor, and has a stable range with an arched carriageway. The White House has 19th century Gothic windows and porch masking an earlier 17th century interior. Bull Cottage and Campden Cottage are attractive contributions to the street, and Morris Cottage has exposed timber framing and dates from the 16th century. Moor Place stands in its own grounds to the west of the High Street.

In the surroundings of Much Hadham are some old and beautiful farmhouses; Yew Tree House at Hadham Cross; Grudds Farm at Green Tye with its moat; Green Tye Farm, a 16th-17th century jettied house, and Kettle Green moated farmhouse with its magnificent barns. Hadham Mill on the River Ash to the south, is a 17th century timber-framed building.

TUDOR COTTAGE, HADHAM HALL

◁ *HALF-TIMBERED COTTAGE, GREAT HORMEAD*

◁ HADHAM HALL, LITTLE HADHAM

HIGH STREET, MUCH HADHAM

THE HALL, MUCH HADHAM

THE CORN EXCHANGE

BISHOP'S STORTFORD

The town is built upon the crossing of four main streets with the market square and the Corn Exchange in the centre, and the church of St Michael alongside the High Street.

The motte and bailey remains of Norman Waytemore Castle stand in Castle Gardens.

The church is predominantly early 15th century and has remarkable misericords in the choir stalls, representing heads of human figures and animals, including an owl, an angel, a swan, a dragon and a swordfish. Corbels supporting the roof timbers have carvings of a monk with a sheaf of corn, a forester with his axe and a cook with a ladle.

The Boar's Head Inn was built in the late 16th century and is a good example of timber framed and plastered building.

The market place is overlooked by Vulliamy's 1828 neo-classical Corn Exchange, and is the hub of the town on market days when it teems with shoppers. Georgian houses abound, restrained brick and plaster detailing perfectly in keeping with their country town setting.

In South Road the Regency villa where Cecil Rhodes was born in 1853 is now a museum devoted to his life and exploits.

THE HALF MOON AND THE CHANTRY *THE BLACK LION* ▷

BENSKINS
THE BLACK LION

THORLEY: HIGH WYCH: GILSTON: WIDFORD

Apart from the isolated church of St James alongside the 15th century Thorley Hall and the village pond, much of *Thorley* has been absorbed into Bishops Stortford. Sir Richard Whittington was Lord of the Manor from 1399 to 1412. The south porch of the church has magnificent zigzag Norman orders, and a fine 12th century font of Purbeck marble.

The flint, red brick and stone-dressed church of *High Wych* was built in 1861 and is a confused amalgam of Gothic forms, interesting only for their ingenuity.

Gilston is split into two distinct parts; the houses and pub, The Plume of Feathers, situated at Pye Corner on the extreme south eastern edge of the county close to the Stort Navigation; and the church and Gilston Park about a mile away to the north. Gilston Park was built in 1852 in Early Tudor style with Gothic details.

The church of St Mary is principally of the 13th century, and is notable for its screen, a well-preserved feature with trefoiled pointed arches and stylised flowers in the spandrels, and for the Tudor stair turret.

Weatherboarded cottages and several fine brick houses comprise the small ridgetop village of *Widford* which looks down on the lush meadows of the River Ash.

The church is isolated on the western edge, and has the grave of Charles Lamb's grandmother who died in 1792 at Blakesware Manor where she worked as housekeeper. The present Blakesware was rebuilt in 1876-79 in neo-Tudor style, and is an elegant composition.

Widfordbury is now a farmhouse but has an early 16th century wall adjoining the churchyard which may have been part of a priory. It has an arched doorway and a moulded plinth. Nearby is a 16th century octagonal dovecote.

THORLEY

BELL STREET, SAWBRIDGEWORTH

SAWBRIDGEWORTH

Built on a square street pattern by the River Stort, *Sawbridgeworth* is one of Hertfordshire's most interesting small towns, although it seems no more than a compact village in scale. The through road and land to the west and south have taken the brunt of suburban expansion. Bell Street, Knight Street and Fair Green contain mainly 16th, 17th and 18th century buildings the best of which are Market House, of two storeys overhung with a gabled wing, and the Red House in Bell Street. Fair Green is surrounded by 18th century houses set in their grounds, including Corner House and Fair Green Lodge. The maltings alongside the Stort and the railway are massive brick buildings with slate roofs.

Burton's Mill, which was half destroyed by fire in 1975, is clad in typical vernacular weather-boarding.

St Mary the Great stands in a green churchyard at the heart of the town and is renowned for its exceptional monuments, ranging from life-size sculptured figures to brasses dating from the 15th century. The Jacobean wall monument to Sir John Leventhorp and his wife was made by William Cure, the Royal Mason, and depicts fourteen kneeling children carved in relief beneath the lady and her husband.

THE SQUARE, SAWBRIDGEWORTH

BLUECOATS YARD, WARE

WARE: WARESIDE

Until the 20th century *Ware* was a prosperous business town, its wealth accrued from trade in malt and corn, but since then Hertford has taken over the county town role and Ware has declined in its shadow. It is this reduced role which has preserved the Georgian character of many of its streets and protected it from wholesale re-development, although West Street has altered radically since F. L. Griggs made drawings in 1900, losing many plastered gables and overhangs in the process. Situated on the River Lea it was a centre for coal and grain business and harnessed coaching trade using the Great North Road.

Along the river banks, painted wooden gazebos terminate the gardens of High Street houses, and create picturesque reflections when seen from the opposite bank or from the bridge.

The High Street is strongly Georgian and has many brick facades interspersed with fragments of earlier timber framing, and some carriageways to former inns. Following the High Street, East and West Streets create parallel shopping lanes with intimate courtyards and gardens opened up by side alleys. One such leads to Bluecoats Yard, where late 17th century almshouses confront Place House across a small courtyard. This former 14th century manor house became the Bluecoat School from 1674 to 1761 before removal to Hertford.

Priory Council Offices at the western end of the High Street have 15th century remains, and the building was a House of the Franciscan Order before the Dissolution. Facing it is the church of St Mary, an embattled construction with a tall five stage tower dating from the 14th century, but sadly over-restored in 1847.

The old Town Hall, built in 1827, is a two storey, eight bay, stock brick building which has fortunately been saved for use as offices. In Baldock Street is The Old Bull's Head, a coaching inn of great character.

Scott's Grotto, built with a garden between 1760 and 1773, by the Quaker poet, John Scott, and one of the finest in England, has recently been extensively restored by the Ware Society.

The village of *Wareside* lies just two miles to the east of Ware in attractive countryside above the River Ash. The church is in the Norman style and was built in 1841. Morley Hall at Butler's Green was originally 17th century, but greatly enlarged during the present century. In Babb's Green remnants of railway stock and architecture stand in a private garden.

GAZEBOS ON THE RIVER LEA, WARE

THE OLD BULL'S HEAD, WARE

PHELPS

HIGH STREET, PUCKERIDGE

PUCKERIDGE: STANDON: ALBURY: PATMORE HEATH

The main street of *Puckeridge* has a few interesting 16th and 17th century houses, marked externally by carriageways, jettied upper floors and some half-timbered construction. To the east at Standon Friars there is a late medieval weatherboarded barn.

Divided by the River Rib, *Standon* parish is made up of scattered settlements. The church of St Mary is unique in Hertfordshire for its detached 15th century tower and for the raised chancel.

The wide main street reminds us that this was once a market town to rival Ware. At Mill End, a Georgian-fronted medieval farmhouse adjoins a weatherboarded water mill and the early 19th century Mill House. South of the village lies The Lordship, a 16th century house by the River Rib and the former home of the Sadleir family, effigies of whom stand in the church. The house was eventually bought by the Duke of Wellington but was partially destroyed by fire in 1927.

Situated between Little Hadham and Furneux Pelham *Albury* is split into three parts: Clapgate, the old centre on high ground with the 13th century church; and Albury End. There is a picturesque village pond, said to be as deep as the church tower is high, on one side of which a 16th century cottage stands next to the church.

There is a Nature Reserve at *Patmore Heath* with cottages dotted around its fringe, and Patmore Hall lies half-concealed near the site of a deserted medieval village in a landscape renowned for its woodlands of hornbeams.

◁ HIGH STREET, WARE

ALBURY

HIGH STREET, STANDON

WEST

CHURCH RUIN, THUNDRIDGE

◁ THE LORDSHIP, STANDON

THUNDRIDGE: WADESMILL: COLLIER'S END: BRAUGHING

Thundridge lies astride the A10 (Ermine Street) at the crossing of the River Rib. Only the west tower of the old parish church survives, hidden by trees and covered with creepers. The Norman doorway shows zigzag and dogtooth decoration. The nearby remains of Thundridge Bury are marked by a tall brick chimney stack forlorn amongst the trees. From here a footpath crosses a bridged island to Fabdens, a Wealdean type house with medieval hall, remarkable for its doorways and its idyllic garden. The village stands apart from this watery and overgrown environment on a small hill near the main road.

Wadesmill has plain Georgian cottages, three inns with a coaching past, and a road bridge supported by 19th century iron columns.

Collier's End lies on the busy A10, but nevertheless retains some charming half-timbered and weather-boarded houses. The small church has some brilliant Art Nouveau woodcarving.

Braughing was important in Roman times, and earthworks at Gatesbury Wood indicate the presence of a substantial Belgic settlement. The River Quin divides Green End from the village proper but a ford provides a road link.

The church of St Mary stands at the centre and is surrounded by timber-framed and pargetted inns and cottages, some with overhangs, dating mostly from the 16th and 17th centuries. The tower and spire of the church are prominent landmarks. This mainly 15th century building has an earlier chancel, a two-storeyed south porch with terrifying gargoyles, and original decorated faces on the corbels.

Nearby Upp Hall to the east has an enormous brick barn with some original pointed-arch openings.

FABDENS, THUNDRIDGE

BRAUGHING VILLAGE STREET

VILLAGE INN, BRAUGHING

HITCHIN, THE MIMRAM AND WELWYN

To the west of the A1 the countryside is hilly where the Chilterns peter out, and villages are generally located in the valleys. Large woodlands speckle the area between Hitchin and Wheathampstead, enhancing the intimacy and enclosure of the landscape. The River Lea defines the southern boundary in a lush and watery environment laced with lakes and reed beds, and the upper reaches of the River Mimram trickle down towards Welwyn through the villages of Whitwell and Codicote, and onwards through green pastures to Hertford. The area is distinguished by several important country houses; at Hexton on the Bedfordshire border; at Knebworth, home of the Lytton Cobbold family; at Mackerye End, a stately Tudor and Jacobean house close to Harpenden; at Shaw's Corner, famous as George Bernard Shaw's home from 1906 to 1950, and at St Paul's Walden Bury with its spectacular gardens.

Hitchin retains much of its medieval street pattern, several fine individual buildings including St Mary's Church and The Priory, and has a thriving market.

The first garden city at nearby Letchworth, the brainchild of Ebenezer Howard, is celebrated for its social and architectural ideas, and for the lead it gave to a generation of internationally respected new towns.

Otherwise villages and greens are made up of farms and dwellings from many periods punctuated by the spikes and towers of their parish churches which denote their position in the landscape.

SUN STREET PASSAGEWAY, HITCHIN

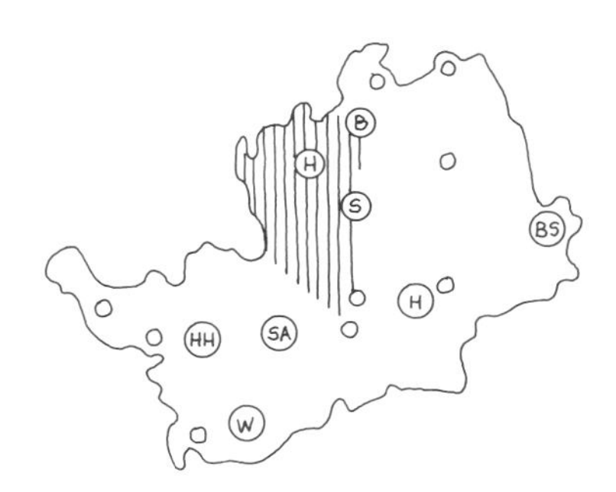

HITCHIN

The medieval shape of the former wool town of *Hitchin* has been preserved despite numerous recent redevelopments, and there are many buildings of architectural merit centred on the church of St Mary and the old market square. Sun Street, Bucklersbury, Tilehouse Street, Bancroft and Bridge Street are the most interesting thoroughfares, with dwellings from the 15th century onwards, a confusion of jumbled rooflines with orange clay tiles and half-timbered gables. Elegant Georgian brick frontages, substantial inns and 19th century chapels and public buildings jostle for space on the narrow streets. Back lanes and alleyways interconnect the main streets and underline the medieval character and intimacy of the town. The Skynner Almshouses in Bancroft are of the late 17th century and elsewhere in this wide curving approach, 18th and 19th century houses have Venetian windows, some fine decorative doorcases with pilasters and columns, and sections of timber framing. On the west side of the market square Sun Street connects to Bridge Street, and contains the Sun Inn, a Georgian building of three storeys and nine bays in blue brick, with a half-timbered range on one side of its inner courtyard, and opposite this are 18th century houses, one with an ornamental brick lintel, and another with wreathed decoration of the cornice frieze. Bridge Street contains a finely preserved row of 15th and 18th century houses, some of which are timber-framed with overhangs, and Tilehouse Street is lined with beautiful houses, timber-framed, herringbone pargetted and stuccoed.

The Priory, for generations the house of the Radcliffe family but now offices, has a Palladian stone facade by Robert Adam dated 1770-77, and in the courtyard are fragments of the Carmelite Priory of Hitchin founded in the early 14th century.

St Mary's Church, with its massively squat tower lies at the centre of the town, the church-yard defined on three sides by alleyways and small shops, and open on the fourth to the new market place beyond spreading willows and the river. Embattled all around, the church has a splendid perpendicular south porch of two storeys with a delicate vaulted ceiling. The nave and battlements are of flint, the chancel chapels of stone, and brick has been used in renovations to both chancel and tower. The screen is a mid-15th century masterpiece, and the interior is crammed with late medieval brasses at its east end, and 18th century wall monuments to the Radcliffe family. Poppy headed stalls, carved ceiling panels and a 15th century stone pulpit are other notable features of this prosperous looking and most attractive church.

ST MARY'S CHURCH TOWER

HALF-TIMBERED HOUSE IN BANCROFT

ST MARY'S CHURCH FROM SQUARE

UP TILEHOUSE STREET ▷

TILEHOUSE STREET HOUSES

GOSMORE VILLAGE

CODICOTE: GOSMORE: GREAT AND LITTLE WYMONDLEY

At the centre of *Codicote* the former 'George and Dragon' dates back to the late 16th century and is a striking jumble of black timber framing and white plastered walls capped by a mellowed clay-tiled roof. Codicote Bury, near the much rebuilt church of St Giles, was built mid-17th century with a stylish pilastered doorway with Ionic columns, frieze and segmental pediment.

This small hamlet of *Gosmore*, just outside Hitchin, has several notable buildings including Maidencroft Manor Farm, and Avenue Farm House, a five bay dwelling dated approximately 1700.

The church of St Mary in *Great Wymondley* has a Norman nave and chancel with interesting carved details, but has been insensitively restored. Earthworks to the east of the church mark the site of a former castle. At *Little Wymondley* is a handsome early 17th century timber-framed Hall with a fine cluster of chimneys, and nearby a 13th century former Augustinian Priory which was transformed into a manorhouse during the late 15th century.

THE FORMER SPIRELLA CORSET FACTORY

LETCHWORTH

In 1903 Ebenezer Howard's great social planning venture began with the building of the world's first Garden City at *Letchworth*. Architects Parker and Unwin prepared designs which incorporated existing routes and landscape features and created a large town square to be enclosed by public buildings, and from which the town's roads radiate.

The old village of Letchworth with its 12th century church and Hall (1620) has been incorporated into the Garden City, but is remote from the town centre.

The vernacular cottage style of much of the housing is generally successful and reflects strong Arts and Crafts leanings in its use of traditional materials and ornamental motifs. Substantial tree planting along the boulevards and enclosing hedges around gardens have fused buildings with landscape and created a mature and comfortable environment. In contrast, the formality and incompleteness of the town centre is deadened by overwhelming neo-Georgian styling.

The former Spirella corset factory is an exciting and witty building of great individuality and power.

Ebenezer Howard tried to stem rural depopulation and reduce urban squalor by creating a safe, clean, socialised world where good wages, low rents and full social provision guaranteed a healthy future in a countryside setting.

◁ *THE FORMER GEORGE AND DRAGON INN: CODICOTE*

WELWYN

Distinct from Welwyn Garden City on the other side of the A1 motorway, *Welwyn* is a Georgian coaching town tucked amongst wooded hills. The River Mimram flows through the town centre bound for the Lea Valley.

Until 1927 the Great North Road passed along High Street and Church Street, accounting for the presence of two coaching inns, the White Hart, and the Wellington, the latter mentioned by Pepys in 1664 under its former name of 'The Swan'.

The church of St Mary stands at the village centre and next to it in Church Street is a half-timbered house dated 1450 which has served many purposes over the centuries including village hall, police station and workhouse.

Mill Lane has a beautiful Georgian Mill house, Assembly Rooms built by Dr Edward Young, poet and rector, who tried to create a spa at Welwyn around a spring located in the rectory gardens.

18th century Danesbury is now a hospital; the Frythe, designed in 1846 by Blore is owned by ICI; Lockleys, also 18th century, just across the A1 is now a part of Sherrardswood School, in the grounds of which a 1st century Roman villa has been excavated, revealing a rectangular colonnaded house, and baths which are now preserved in a vault under the motorway and occasionally open to the public.

Van Gogh's sister taught at Welwyn from 1875 to 1876 and was visited by the painter who walked out from London.

CHURCHYARD COTTAGE, WELWYN

THE WHITE HART, OLD WELWYN

WHEATHAMPSTEAD: KING'S WALDEN

Wheathampstead is remarkable for several reasons, although the High Street possesses very few buildings of architectural interest. The site of a Belgic settlement, it was probably the headquarters of Cassivellaunus who led his tribes unsuccessfully against Julius Caesar in 54BC. Devil's Dyke and the Slad earthworks denote the importance of the site.

The church of St Helen is a large flint building with a dominant crossing tower topped by an impressive lead broach spire. Largely built during the 13th and 14th centuries on older foundations, it has exciting stone tracery in the transept windows.

Apsley Cherry Garrard, the Polar explorer who was in Scott's last expedition to the South Pole in 1910, lived in nearby Lamer House, and a statue of him can be seen in the church. Where the High Street crosses the River Lea the 16th-17th century mill and the timber framed Bull Hotel make a picturesque group.

Close to Wheathampstead are two important houses. At Mackerye End a fine Jacobean fronted mansion dated 1665 with Dutch gables and elaborate chimney stacks, is set at the end of a central driveway behind trimmed hedges and green lawns. At the rear of the house is a timber framed section possibly dating from the previous century. It was visited by and written about by Charles Lamb.

Water End Farm to the south east of Wheathampstead is a Jacobean manor house built in 1610; a solid brick building with distinctive mullioned windows, overlooking a delightful ford on the River Lea. It is reputed to be the birthplace of Sarah, Duchess of Marlborough.

At *King's Walden* a William Morris stained glass window dated 1867 depicting three archangels is the outstanding feature of St Mary's church, which stands enclosed by thick yew hedges as the lane to Luton drops steeply away under an archway of oak trees.

The Bury is a neo-Georgian house built in 1972 on the site of the 1890's 'Elizabethan' mansion.

THE MILL AND THE BULL, WHEATHAMPSTEAD

MACKERYE END, NEAR WHEATHAMPSTEAD ▷

WATER END FARM, NEAR WHEATHAMPSTEAD

OLD ST LAWRENCE RUINS

AYOT ST LAWRENCE: AYOT ST PETER: LEMSFORD

At *Ayot St Lawrence* the ruined and overgrown church of St Lawrence was made so by the Lord of the Manor, Sir Lionel Lyde, when he built the classical New St Lawrence designed by Nicholas Revett in 1778 in the form of a Greek temple and used materials from the old church. The wrought iron gate to the old churchyard is especially beautiful. George Bernard Shaw, the dramatist, lived in the New Rectory, called Shaw's Corner, from 1906 until his death in 1950, and whilst here wrote such well known plays at Pygmalion and Saint Joan. The house is now a National Trust museum kept as Shaw left it, and is open for viewing.

The village has some attractive half-timbered cottages and the Brocket Arms, a quaint inn opposite the churchyard. Ayot House appears to be a Queen Anne building and the old Manor House nearby is of Tudor construction with a 17th century front. Bride Hall about one mile to the south of the village is a brick Jacobean manor house with weatherboard barns.

Ayot St Peter village green is divided by tree-lined avenues and surrounded by cottages and elegant houses, notable amongst which are Ayot Place, a 1615 farmhouse with timber-framed wings and a minstrel's gallery in the hall, and Ayotbury, an orderly house built in 1672 with later additions.

Lemsford. Brocket Hall by James Paine with Adam interiors stands magnificently above the River Lea with its spectiacular bridge providing a dramatic introduction on the approach through the park.

GREAT OFFLEY: LITTLE OFFLEY: KIMPTON: ST IPPOLLITTS: ST PAUL'S WALDEN

The Hitchin to Luton road cuts a vicious swathe through the hillside close to *Great Offley,* but simultaneously protects the village from heavy traffic. At the village crossroads Westbury Farm dates from 1600 and is half-timbered and plastered. A 17th century dove-cote stands in the farmyard. Offley Place, said to be designed by Robert Smirke (1806-1818) is a five-bay mansion.

The church of St Mary Magdalene has medieval aisles and a nave of flint and limestone, but the brick tower is in the early 19th century Gothic style. The font is a beautiful example of 14th century tracery panels.

At *Little Offley,* a late Tudor brick manor house with an Elizabethan wooden fireplace stands in leafy grounds at the end of a lane.

The long village street of *Kimpton* is flanked by late Victorian houses and some earlier brick cottages. At its eastern end the green is enclosed by terraced cottages, and leads to the church of St Peter and St Paul, which has a two-storeyed porch, medieval screens and benches with carved poppyheads.

At *St Ippollitts,* the church, a Victorian school and a former inn are grouped around a small hilltop green within sight of the Hitchin to Codicote road. The church was rebuilt in the 1870's but has traces of an original 11th century structure and features striking corbel sculptures of a monk, a bishop, a nun, a lady and a man with unusual headgear.

Set in a delightful wooded and undulating landscape, the small village of *St Paul's Walden* has a remarkable church with an English Baroque chancel designed and built by Edward Gilbert in 1727, with a barrel-vaulted ceiling, walls of moulded plaster painted green and white, and a sumptuous nave screen with columns, entablature, arches and candelabra on the cornice. Queen Elizabeth, The Queen Mother's family home is at The Bury, and a plaque in the church commemorates her baptism here in 1900. The lovely 18th century formal and woodland gardens are often open for charity.

WESTBURY FARM, GREAT OFFLEY

◁ *THE BRIDGE, BROCKET HALL, LEMSFORD*

COTTAGES AT KIMPTON

ST PAUL'S WALDEN BURY ▷

ST IPPOLLITTS CHURCH

THE TANNERY, WHITWELL

WHITWELL: BREACHWOOD GREEN: BENDISH

Although having no church, *Whitwell* is in the parish of St Paul's Walden. The High Street is lined with an interesting blend of half-timbered Elizabethan houses, brick fronted Georgian and Victorian villas and two fine inns, 'The Eagle and Child' and 'The Bull'. A quiet lane leads down to the River Mimram which flows unobtrusively past richly overgrown private gardens.

Breachwood Green lies in rolling countryside to the east of Luton at the heart of a complex network of narrow lanes. The Baptist Chapel, built in 1904, contains John Bunyan's pulpit, and has a traceried window above the doorway and some elaborate ironmongery.

Tiny *Bendish* is close to Whitwell and on the same ridge as Breachwood Green, and supports a small pub at its heart.

PIRTON: HEXTON: LANGLEY: HOLWELL: WILLIAN: PRESTON

At *Pirton* the oval shaped remains of a motte and bailey castle known as Toot Hill enclose the Norman church of St Mary, whose tower and transepts collapsed in 1874. The tower was rebuilt and crowned with a Hertfordshire spike. Cottages and an inn abut the village green, and several neighbouring manor houses make this an interesting place to visit. Old Hall, Hammonds Farm, Rectory Farm and High Down (1599) are the principal houses, but Pirton Grange at some distance from the village on a moated island on the Bedfordshire border, has a unique atmosphere created partly by its inaccessibility and partly by its faded appearance. The timber-framed gatehouse bridges the moat and leads through a flower-filled garden to the shell-hooded front door. A polished brass bell pull is the only outward sign of maintenance, but the interior is a treasure house of quirky details and eccentric adaptations carried out over the past three centuries. The Grange is a private residence and not open to the public.

The Iron Age hill fort of Ravensburgh lies in the Barton Hills above *Hexton* and is spectacularly sited overlooking the lowlands of Bedfordshire to the north, and overgrown with stands of beech trees. It is a nostalgic location and of great archeological interest. The village church of St Faith probably has 13th century beginnings, but was heavily restored during the 19th century under the patronage of the de Latour family who lived at the mid-Victorian manor house. In 1846 the village pump, which stands on the crossroads, was erected by Caroline de Latour, and is now an attractive street lamp-cum-signpost.

Langley is notable for houses designed by Sir Edwin Lutyens; Langley End, Hill End, and Hill End Farm.

A minute pub, 'The Farmer's Boy' stands on the eastern edge looking across to Newton Wood and Stevenage. A beautiful lane winds down to Hitch Wood from Shelley Green.

THE FOX INN, PIRTON

The unremarkable village of *Holwell* has an 1832 Rectory, a school dated 1841, and some Tudor style almshouses built in 1832 and 1885. Old Ramerick to the north has a fine seven bay, two storey William and Mary front.

Preston village green has a well with its iron mechanism under an octagonal roof, and is surrounded by neat houses with flower-filled gardens. The church of St Martin, built in 1900, was modern for its time, and contains details reminiscent of the work of the architect Voysey.

PIRTON GRANGE ▷

FORMER VILLAGE PUMP, HEXTON

BALDOCK, THE BEANE AND HERTFORD

This area includes the substantial compact old towns of Baldock and Hertford in contrast to the sprawling new towns of Stevenage and Welwyn Garden City.

A close-grained network of narrow lanes, many with passing places, permeates the intervening countryside and connects farm to farm and hamlet to hamlet, occasionally focussing upon a larger village at a significant crossing point. Roman Stane Street crossed this part of the county clinging to the higher ground between Baldock and Puckeridge and linking the Great North Road and Ermine Street. There is archeological evidence that several villages in the north eastern part were abandoned during the 14th century due to combinations of poor weather and recurrent plagues.

Benington, Westmill and Cottered are especially picturesque, but Graveley, Cromer, Weston and Walkern also have fine individual buildings, and at Tewin stands Queen Hoo Hall, one of the finest small Elizabethan houses in England.

The River Beane flows southwards from Walkern, creating in its wake a glistening trail of reflections amongst the willows and green fields. Punctuated by bridges and weirs the river copes with roads, railways and occasional villages whilst competing for space in the flood plain, as it wends its way to Hertford and joins the River Lea.

THATCHING, COTTERED

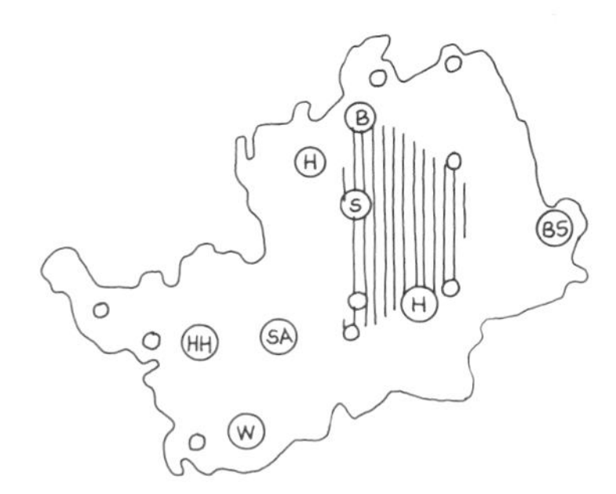

BALDOCK

Baldock lies in the lee of a steep wooded hillside, and is distinguished by the prominent tower and spike of St Mary's Church. At one time an important coaching town on the Great North Road, its prosperity grew during the 18th century, and this is reflected in several fine Georgian houses and large coaching inns, some of which retain their heavy oak carriage-way doors. The church stands at the crossing in the centre, and is largely of the 14th century, and strongly reminiscent of St Mary's in Ashwell.

The half-timbered 'Bull's Head Inn' in Church Street and Wynne's Almshouses in the High Street date from the 17th century. Another remarkable building is the 1853 Methodist Chapel in White Horse Street with its brick gabled front and two tall octagonal buttresses carrying lanterns. In Hitchin Street close to the church is the rectory designed by Butterfield in 1870-73 and built in red brick with a timber-framed gable. Other fine houses with overhangs, timber-framed sections, pedimented doorcases, pilasters and decorative brickwork are to be found along this street.

CHURCH STREET

ST MARY'S CHURCHYARD

CHURCH STREET CARRIAGEWAY

CROMER MILL

CROMER: COTTERED: CLOTHALL: WALKERN: BASSUS GREEN

At the south end of *Cromer* is an attractive 16th century half-timbered building with overhangs and gables. The post mill is the only one remaining in Hertfordshire, and is a striking white-painted weatherboarded structure with intact sails, supported on a red brick round house, and was completely restored by Hertfordshire Building Preservation Trust between 1967 and 1970.

The thatched, tiled and weatherboarded cottages and inns of *Cottered* cluster around a series of shaded greens laced along the Baldock to Buntingford road. The church, with a large aisleless nave, has a fine wall painting of St Christopher. The Lordship is a part 15th and part 17th century manor house and has the remnant of a moat and a dovecote.

A tiny village off the Baldock to Buntingford road, *Clothall* has a small 14th century church with beautiful stained glass chancel windows depicting Christ, the Virgin, and the Apostles in medallions, and incorporating flowers and birds added in the 15th century. The drawings of birds of the field are unique in England and worth a special journey. Clothall House, the former rectory, is a fine Georgian brick building.

Situated on the Cottered to Stevenage road *Walkern* is strung out and much developed in recent times, but has several fine country houses including Walkern Hall at the north end, set back across a field and behind a screen of yew trees; Manor Farm, a Georgian house with an octagonal dovecote and pond; and Rooks Nest Farm. The church lies beyond the ford on the River Beane and has interesting Norman remnants in the south doorway, part of the arcade and in a large blocked window in the south aisle. The marble effigy of a knight with his face hidden by the visor of his helmet dates from the 13th century, and in the south side of the wall above the arcade is the remains of a rood, or crucifix, in late Saxon style, showing a head in relief and a flat draped body surrounded by a stone frame.

At *Bassus Green* snug farmhouses amongst fruit trees accompanied by thatched and weather-boarded barns define this remote crossroads.

At nearby Walkern Bury Farm the earthworks of King's Bailey reveal an oval enclosure with bank, ditch and traces of a mound.

◁ *MANOR FARM AND DOVECOTE, WALKERN*

CROMER FARM

BASSUS GREEN FARM BUILDINGS

WOOD END COTTAGE, THE MUNDENS

LUFFENHALL: MOOR GREEN: GREAT AND LITTLE MUNDEN

In the scattered hamlet of *Luffenhall* Walnut Tree Farm is an excellent example of a medieval hall-house with a jettied cross-wing. Whitehall is a beautiful half-timbered house with an unusual cloister and verandah and a rich red clay-tiled roof.

Moor Green is a loose collection of farms scattered around a large common green to the east of Ardeley, a windswept and exposed location hard by the line of Roman Stane Street.

Situated on an open upland landscape which in medieval times was abandoned by the peasants for the sheltered valleys below, *Great Munden* is a collection of farming communities of which Nasty is the largest. The recently closed church of St Nicholas, started in the 12th century, has ogee-headed aisle recesses and a fine stone reredos with ogee niches.

The Plough Inn on the road to Dane End has a theatre organ removed from the Gaumont, Finchley. Dane End is the largest settlement in the parish of Little Munden and its winding High Street has a homely pub, several attractive cottages, the White House (1830) and Dane End House, an early 19th century mansion.

The Church of All Saints, *Little Munden* stands apart from Dane End together with its rectory and a school, and is mainly 14th century, although traces of Norman work remain in the north aisle.

Other hamlets in the Mundens cluster are Haultwick, Green End, Levens Green, Rush Green and Wood End.

◁ *WHITEHALL FARM, LUFFENHALL*

DANE END, THE MUNDENS

NASTY: SACOMBE: WESTMILL: CHERRY GREEN: WESTON

Nasty is close to Great Munden, and lies in a hollow in the landscape, its charming weather-boarded and thatched cottages somewhat contradicting its name.

The former rectory of *Sacombe* is a very attractive 15th-17th century timber-framed house with wooden mullioned windows and a jettied upper floor.

Inside the little Church of St Catherine there are sculptures by Rysbrack (1758) and Flaxman (1815).

The way in which *Westmill's* cottages group around the small green with the church tower rising over the rooftops, makes this charming village one of the most picturesque in the county. A strong sweep of pollarded limes and a large chestnut tree shading the inn enrich the peaceful rural atmosphere.

The church was over-restored during the 19th century but has Anglo-Saxon remnants, rare stone angels carrying flaming torches around the tower door, and medieval choir stalls with poppyheads.

To the east the River Rib trickles through beautiful water meadows and stands of trees which screen the village from nearby Roman Ermine Street.

Buttonsnap, the cottage inherited by Charles Lamb in 1812 is at *Cherry Green,* its massive thatched roof dwarfing the plastered walls beneath. At Wakeley to the west of the village are the earthworks of a deserted medieval village.

The church of Holy Trinity at *Weston* has a Norman crossing with intact arches and lower tower, and the north transept has two Norman windows. It was heavily restored in 1840 when the chancel was rebuilt in neo-Norman style.

The grave of 'Jack O'Legs', a local 'giant', is reputedly between two stones by the church gate. He was a kind of Robin Hood character who, according to legend, robbed the rich to aid the poor. The local lanes twist about to connect Weston with Warren Green and Hall Green.

THE RED LION, WESTON

WEATHERBOARDED COTTAGE, NASTY

WESTMILL GREEN

BUTTONSNAP COTTAGE, CHERRY GREEN

ARDELEY: ASPENDEN

Ardeley is notable for its picturesque green surrounded by whitewashed thatched cottages and village hall, created in 1917 by the Lord of the Manor. Ardeley Bury stands apart and is a much altered late Tudor manor house. The church of St Lawrence has a rood loft with painted rood and rood canopy designed by F. C. Eden who also designed the buildings around the green.

Aspenden is built on both sides of a stream and a long winding village street, in which a variety of cottages and inns, pargetted, thatched and painted, culminates in the lovely hilltop church. The south porch has pre-Raphaelite stained glass by Morris and Company (1920). Bishop Seth Ward was born here in 1618 and later became Bishop of Salisbury and Chancellor of the Order of the Garter.

TREE ON THE GREEN, ARDELEY

ARDELEY VILLAGE GREEN

KNEBWORTH PARK OAKS

OLD KNEBWORTH: KNEBWORTH

Old Knebworth is a village of almshouses and lodges hugging the edge of Knebworth Park to the west of the A1 Motorway. *Knebworth* grew up separately around the station and the Great North Road.

Knebworth House is a 19th century remodelling of the 15th century house and chiefly the concept of the owner, Sir Edward Bulwer-Lytton, whose family are still in occupation and open the property to the public on a major scale. The exterior of the house with its turrets and bizarre gargoyles is an over elaborate and highly romantic neo-Gothic creation, but the Great Hall, all that remains of the Tudor building, retains sections of the plastered ceiling, panelling and a magnificent oak screen.

Much of the garden was designed by Sir Edward Lutyens who was also responsible for work in the village; St Martin's Church (1914), the Golf Club House (1908) and Homewood (1900) which is a fine example of his early domestic style with weatherboarded gables, and several other cottages. The church of St Mary and St Thomas stands in the park of Knebworth House and has an interesting 15th century tower with gargoyles, a Norman chancel arch and outstanding monuments to the Lyttons.

◁ *ASPENDEN COTTAGE*

HIGH STREET, BUNTINGFORD

BUNTINGFORD

Flanking the London to Cambridge road, *Buntingford* was an important coaching town, with its long High Street, once a part of Roman Ermine Street.

Several Tudor buildings with overhangs, and elegant Georgian town houses stand side by side with early 19th century cottages and former coaching inns, complete with large carriageway arches.

The Seth Ward Almshouses built in 1684 and the unusual brick church of St Peter, completed in 1626, flank the wide space at the southern end of the High Street, where large mature trees create an attractive focal point to the town. The finishing touches are supplied by a covered water pump and a 16th century turret clock.

The ruined church of St Bartholomew once belonged to the deserted village of Layston, and served Buntingford until the end of the 16th century, but now lies open to the skies, nostalgically deserted in its overgrown graveyard, half a mile to the east of the town centre.

◁ *KNEBWORTH HOUSE*

SETH WARD ALMSHOUSES, BUNTINGFORD

FOX AND DUCK INN, BUNTINGFORD

STEVENAGE: GRAVELEY: ASTON

13th century St Nicholas' Church stood at the centre of the original medieval village of *Stevenage*, but the Georgian Old Town moved to take advantage of the coaching trade on the Great North Road, and this elegant broad main street survives despite the development of the New Town after the Second World War: The White Lion, The Cromwell Hotel, The Two Diamonds and The Yorkshire Grey are prominent surviving inns. At the north end the High Street opens out to form Bowling Green, a triangular space surrounded by picturesque cottages, and Tudor Alleyn's School. The Grange, an early Georgian building, was formerly The Swan Inn, where Samuel Pepys once stayed. E. M. Forster spent his childhood in Stevenage, and he modelled Hilton of 'Howards End' on a house situated on the Weston Road.

The New Town started in 1946, and is a thoughtful blend of public and private housing planned to take advantage of the natural features of the site and to incorporate existing farming hamlets as neighbourhoods. The centre has a pedestrian precinct and in its time was considered advanced, although the use of concrete and utilitarian building materials has bequeathed a rather tawdry legacy. Segregated cycle routes are also an important integral feature of the planning concept, and together with a generous landscaping philosophy which structures and softens the built form of the town, Stevenage makes a significant contribution to modern town planning development.

When the Great North Road passed through *Graveley* 'The George and Dragon' and 'The Rose and Crown' were important coaching inns. They now form part of a group of buildings close to the village pond which is overlooked by several attractive dwellings, including Gothic House with its 18th century bay-window corbelled out over a central doorway.

The church and Graveley Hall Farm (17th century) lie at the end of a lane branching off the main road and can be approached by footpath across the fields. The farm is an appealing brick building with large dark-painted weatherboarded barns enclosing a gravelled courtyard. Half a mile to the east the lane reaches the deserted village of Chesfield where the remains of St Etheldreda's church stand forlornly next to Chesfield Manor Farm.

Stevenage sprawls to the west but *Aston* retains its separate identity and has a part-13th century church with a fine brass commemorating John Kent, a steward to Edward VI, Queen Mary and Queen Elizabeth I. Aston Bury is half a mile to the south, a Jacobean brick mansion with remains of an earlier Tudor house.

RUINED CHURCH OF ST ETHELDREDA, CHESFIELD

OLD TOWN, STEVENAGE

CHURCH MANOR AND BARNS, GRAVELEY

FORMER COACHING INNS, GRAVELEY ▷

GREENE KING

GOTHIC HOUSE, GRAVELEY

COTTAGE DOOR, BENINGTON

BENINGTON

Although close to burgeoning Stevenage, *Benington* remains surprisingly intact, sited on the ridge around a classic village green, and surrounded by timber framed cottages, St Peter's Church, The Bell Inn and The Lordship manor house on the site of a Norman castle. The Keep and fragments of walls remain, and a neo-Norman gate house was constructed from remnants in 1832.

Benington was once the seat of the Saxon Kings of Mercia and the site of a council held here in 850AD to decide upon defensive action against invading Vikings.

Notable buildings are the Old Rectory (1637), Benington Bury (17th century), and The Old House, a 16th century timber-framed dwelling.

St Peter's is essentially a late 13th to early 14th century church with a 15th century Hertfordshire spike. Its best features are a sedilia in the chancel and the north chancel chapel.

The Bell
GREENE KING

◁ *THE BELL, BENINGTON*

ST MARY'S CHURCH, STAPLEFORD

WELWYN GARDEN CITY: DIGSWELL: STAPLEFORD: WATTON-AT-STONE

Founded in 1919 by a private company, *Welwyn Garden City* was planned by Ebenezer Howard, and subsequently replanned after the Second World War by Louis de Soissons for a revised population of 50,000. Tree-lined boulevards and numbing neo-Georgian red brick architecture dominate, but there are several adventurous factory buildings, in particular one for the Shredded Wheat Company (1925) and for Roche Products (1938-40).

The forty lofty arches of *Digswell* Viaduct carry the main line from Kings Cross to Edinburgh and were built by Lewis Cubitt between 1848 and 1850 using about 6,000 'navvies' and five million bricks.

Digswell House, by S. Wyatt features a full-height colonnaded portico with Ionic capitals. The village has some charming old cottages clustered beneath the viaduct.

The nave of St Mary's Church, *Stapleford,* dates from 1150AD and has a Norman north doorway. The tower has a distinctive octagonal timber stage and spire built in 1874.

The long High Street of *Watton-at-Stone* has well maintained Victorian almshouses, a few pargetted buildings and a 19th century cast-iron pump. Watton Place, now the Doctors' Surgery, is medieval in origin and is probably the oldest house. The embattled church of St Andrew and St Mary overlooks the roof-tops from its elevated position away from the village. Woodhall Park, by Thomas Leverton, built in 1777, is a very fine classical house standing in attractive parkland sloping down to the River Beane, and has an elegant stable block built around a central courtyard at some distance apart from the main house.

At *Frogmore* The Hall is a red brick neo-Gothic mansion with square tower. Alongside the A602 is a charming white neo-Gothic lodge with crenellated battlements.

DIGSWELL VIADUCT

WOODHALL PARK, WATTON-AT-STONE

BRAMFIELD: BULL'S GREEN: DATCHWORTH: TEWIN

St Thomas a Becket's name heads the list of rectors at *Bramfield's* church of St Andrew, and much later he went on to become Chancellor of England in 1155 and Archbishop of Canterbury in 1162, culminating in his murder in 1170 by King Henry II's knights.

The tiny hamlet of *Bull's Green* lies between Bramfield and Datchworth and is a cluster of houses, a farm and The Horns, an attractive country pub.

A collection of 'greens' amongst a tangle of narrow lanes culminates in *Datchworth Green* where an ancient whipping post surrounded by an iron grill stands as a grim reminder of past customs.

All Saints' Church has a 12th century nave with later additions, and features a High Perpendicular font, and some delicate floriated capitals on Purbeck marble shafts in the north aisle arcade.

The Elizabethan Queen Hoo Hall at *Tewin* is one of the architectural gems of the county and its mellow brick walls overlook an exquisite garden to the south, and a sublime rural landscape beyond. It is a private house and not open to the public but can be viewed from an adjacent bridleway. The village is undistinguished and the church is remarkable only for the churchyard tomb of Anne Grimston (d.1713) whose grave has a tree growing from it, lifting the tomb into the air. She had declared that an after life was as likely as a tree sprouting from her grave.

QUEEN HOO HALL, TEWIN

POSTERN GATE, HERTFORD CASTLE

HERTFORD: BENGEO

Hertford is the county town and has a long recorded history going back beyond the Norman Conquest. In 673AD the first National Synod was held here which Bishops of the five ancient kingdoms attended. The Saxon stronghold was replaced by a Norman Castle after the Conquest, of which only the motte survives. The main existing feature is the Gatehouse which was built in 1461 between the inner and outer baileys and now serves the Town Council as offices.

Fore Street is the main thoroughfare of the town and contains exceptional examples of pargetting in a row of 17th century buildings opposite the Salisbury Arms, itself a late 16th and early 17th century courtyard inn with a fine Jacobean staircase and an overhanging upper floor.

The former Green Dragon Hotel on Parliament Square has some extraordinary brown terracotta work (1903) with bold relief lettering.

Christ's Hospital School was founded in 1683 and completed in 1695. The gateway to Fore Street with its 1721 Bluecoat boys' statues and the original girls' school building of 1778, also with statues in niches in the facade, are the only remaining buildings of the period. Other later buildings have been converted into offices since the school closed in 1985.

James Adam designed the Shire Hall in 1768. A severe yellow brick building in the town centre, it has a fine top-lit rotunda on the upper floor.

In Bull Plain a small museum explains the history of the town, and this street leads to the Maltings where the Rivers Beane and Lea meet and where colourfully painted barges are often moored. Across the river lies Hartham Common and the road to Bengeo.

A hilltop community north of Hertford, *Bengeo* has a rare and extremely fine Norman village church. St Leonard's is one of the oldest buildings in Hertfordshire and one of only three with an apse. Bengeo Hall is a brick mid-Georgian house with a dovecote and mellow garden walls.

◁ *MALTINGS ON THE BEANE*

THE SALISBURY ARMS HOTEL

PARLIAMENT SQUARE

THE FORMER CHRIST'S HOSPITAL SCHOOL

ST LEONARD'S CHURCH, BENGEO

ST ALBANS, HATFIELD AND THE LEA VALLEY

This area comprises the district around St Albans and the land fringing London from Broxbourne in the east to the M1 in the west.

On the eastern edge of the area the River Lea forms a series of reservoirs and lakes bordered by continuous and often tedious development, where main line railway, dual carriageway roads and light industrial factories vie with homes for breathing space.

Surprisingly, the land to the south of Hertford remains heavily wooded and is peppered with delightful villages dispersed amongst the lanes and folds of the countryside.

At Hatfield one of England's finest Jacobean houses stands on the site of a great Tudor Palace only a small part of which remains, and is surrounded by stately parkland with ancient trees and elegant vistas.

Historic St Albans is one of the most intriguing cities in the country with its Roman remains, its cathedral and its sumptuous combination of medieval streets and stylish houses.

THE OLD FIGHTING COCKS INN, ST ALBANS

ST ALBANS

From the ruins of Roman Verulamium across the River Ver, the Cathedral and Abbey Church of Saint Alban rears above modest city rooftops, a symbol of an important past. Before the Dissolution the huge Abbey belonged to the Benedictines, and was amongst the greatest in England. The remains of the monastery have largely disappeared, and the church was designated a Cathedral only in 1877. It stands on the site of Saint Alban's execution in 209AD, although remains of the original shrine have vanished, and the present building dates from the time of Abbot Paul of Caen between 1077AD and 1088AD.

Roman bricks from Verulamium were used extensively to build the Norman church and their dark colour gives the tower a sombre appearance. The interior is lightened by plastered surfaces, some of which have medieval wall paintings, and by pale limestone walls. The nave was extended westwards during the 12th century, culminating in the completion of the west front in 1230AD. Of the many monuments, the centrepiece is the Shrine of Saint Alban, which has been reassembled from the 14th century original, and the Watching Loft, which is a raised timber platform designed to allow a custodian to keep a watchful eye on the Shrine.

Fishpool Street, St Peter's Street and Holywell Hill radiate from the hub of the town, and the finest of these is arguably Fishpool Street which begins at the green in front of the cathedral and winds sinuously down to the river and Kingsbury Watermill. It is lined with houses and inns from Tudor to Victorian times, and features raised pavements, structural timber-framing, plastered overhangs, carved doorcases, carriageways and elegant brick facades. Kingsbury Watermill has been converted into a restaurant and a museum, and nestles in a lush and watery setting.

St Michael's Church on the site of Verulamium has Saxon flint walls incorporating Roman tiles, and a Norman aisle. An effigy of Sir Francis Bacon reminds us that his body was brought here in 1626, for he lived at nearby Gorhambury.

Verulamium was founded in 43AD, and was Roman Britain's chief city. Remains of flint walling and tiles define the theatre, a hypercaust and a garrison dwelling. Watling Street joins St Michael's to St Stephen's church across the site. Excavations are well displayed in the Verulamium Museum, which includes mosaics and wall paintings.

DOWN FISHPOOL STREET

THE CATHEDRAL ▷

THE NORMAN NAVE

KINGSBURY WATERMILL

ACROSS THE VER TO ST MICHAEL'S HILL

THE CLOCK TOWER

HARPENDEN: LONDON COLNEY: SANDRIDGE: CHILDWICK GREEN

With its villas lining the edges of a large open common, *Harpenden* has a very distinctive 'Metroland' feel to it. The tree-lined High Street is lively and contains domestic buildings dating from the 16th century to the present day.

The Old House, formerly the Bull Inn, is a fine timber-framed building, and Bowers House has an 11 bay Queen Anne facade masking early 16th century construction. Rothamsted Manor has a mid-17th century front with Dutch gables and a cupola similar to that at Mackerye End. The Manor is now a student hall of residence for the Rothamsted Experimental Station or Agricultural Research Centre, which Sir John Barnett Lawes, who was born here in 1814, helped to found. Parts of the Manor are actually pre-17th century and are incorporated into subsequent rebuildings. The interiors feature linenfold panelling in the hallway, Jacobean fireplaces, 16th century wall painting, and a stone-carved fireplace from Rawdon House, Hoddesdon. Within the grounds of the Manor are the remains of a Roman shrine containing burials and an altar foundation.

Harpenden Hall and the Moat House Hotel on the south side of the common are fine 17th century houses with elegant 18th century additions and 20th century conversion work.

All Saints' Pastoral Centre at *London Colney* marks the spot where Saint Alban was captured before his martyrdom, and thereby became a focus for pilgrims. It was built in 1899 as an Anglican convent, and in 1927 the chapel was added, and together they make up an impressive group of buildings. Salisbury Hall, a most tranquil moated house, stands sheltered by tall trees, and was the secret birthplace of the Second World War Mosquito aircraft. Nell Gwynne is reputed to have lived in the cottage alongside the moat.

SALISBURY HALL, LONDON COLNEY

St Leonard's Church at *Sandridge* is a remarkable building with late 12th century nave arcades, chancel masonry using Roman bricks, and a 12th century font and pulpit. A stone screen incorporating the chancel arch was built in the late 14th century.

Childwick Green is a mid-Victorian model village set in the grounds of Childwickbury, a large late 17th century mansion two miles north of St Albans. A few small houses cluster around an immaculate, white-railed green, and facing this is the church of St Mary by Giles Gilbert Scott, built in 1867.

COACH LANE COTTAGE, HARPENDEN

HATFIELD

At the end of the 15th century Bishop Morton built the Palace at Hatfield, separated from the church of St Etheldreda by the Great North Road which ran down Fore Street and along Park Street. The houses of the town clustered around this nucleus of Church and Palace. Both Mary Tudor and Elizabeth I spent part of their childhood virtually imprisoned at the Palace, the only remains of which are the Great Hall and some attached buildings, which survived Robert Cecil's building of Hatfield House on adjacent land between 1607 and 1612 to the designs of Robert Lyminge and Inigo Jones. Hatfield House is indisputedly the finest mansion in Hertfordshire and a remarkable tour de force of design for the period.

It is the seat of the Cecil family, which produced one of England's Prime Ministers in the 3rd Marquess. The principal features of the house are the brick-built wings with their corner towers, and the stone-built loggia between them, comprising round-headed arches separated by Roman Doric pilasters and decorated with strapwork screens.

The clock tower by Inigo Jones was destroyed by fire in 1988, but has been reconstructed using photographs and drawings. The north facade of the house is somewhat forbidding in character with its mass of largely unrelieved brickwork and severely mullioned windows, and has a decidedly modern appearance, shorn as it is of the original end gables and coats of arms, not to mention ivy wall creepers.

The Grand Staircase by Bucke displays the finest Jacobean wood carving of 1612, and echoes the craftsmanship in the screen of the Great Hall with its projecting upper gallery. In 1879 Hatfield House became one of the first homes to be lit by newly patented Edison-Swan electric light bulbs.

The formal gardens are made up of cloisters of trellised lime trees, flower beds with a fountain, and walled grassy lawns with walkways. Beyond the formal gardens open parkland is surrounded by woodlands, and several ancient oaks stand grotesquely deformed and twisted with age.

The River Lea flows through what was once a great vineyard on the northern edge of the park, where a castellated brick wall, a tower and an early 19th century summer house survive. Formal vistas stretch from Hatfield House out into the park, defining and emphasising the grandeur of the design concept.

Fore Street is a beautiful sloping street of stepped Georgian houses and former coaching inns. At the foot of the hill on the corner of Park Street is the timber-framed Eight Bells Inn with its sunken stone-flagged floor and intimately divided interior, which Charles Dickens immortalised as the refuge of Bill Sikes in Oliver Twist.

Hatfield New Town was established in 1948 and has several interesting buildings, amongst which are the De Havilland factory, and the swimming pool with its hyperbolic paraboloid roof.

THE EIGHT BELLS INN

FORE STREET

◁ *HATFIELD HOUSE, SOUTH FRONT*

THE OLD PALACE

HERTFORD HEATH: GREAT AMWELL: NORTHAW: BAYFORD: HERTINGFORDBURY

Haileybury College is the principal building at *Hertford Heath,* and was opened in 1809 as a college for the Honourable East India Company. William Wilkins was the architect of the stone south facade with yellow brick buildings formed around a quadrangle. At the closure of the Company and of the College in 1858 the place became derelict for a while, until reopened as a public school in 1862. The chapel by Blomfield with its gigantic dome, prominent for miles around was consecrated in 1877.

It was in *Great Amwell* that Sir Hugh Myddelton founded the New River Works, designed to bring fresh water supplies to London. He is commemorated in an inscribed monumental urn erected 200 years later by Robert Mylne on an island in the river Lea to the north of the church and the water gardens with the landscaping are of a very high order.

The church of St John the Baptist has a Norman apse and a chancel with intact 11th century features.

Also a commuter village, *Northaw* has an alien rock-faced late Victorian church and several good Georgian houses.

In the village of *Bayford* Bayfordbury has a 25 bay white stuccoed facade facing an ornamental lake and was built in two periods c1760 and c1810.

Bayford House has beautiful outbuildings and there are very old cottages around the duck pond.

A small village on a triangle of lanes *Hertingfordbury* has a fine church and some distinctive houses. The landscaped park surrounding what was once Panshanger was designed by Repton who used the bridge over the river Mimram as a centrepiece.

THE NEW RIVER, GREAT AMWELL

RYE HOUSE GATEHOUSE, HODDESDON

HODDESDON: BROXBOURNE: CHESHUNT: WALTHAM CROSS

The town of *Hoddesdon* is now part of the sprawl extending along the west bank of the River Lea from London to Hertford, but retains some of the old inns, The Golden Lion, The Swan and The Bell, and Rawdon House, built in 1622 and now converted into offices. The brick gatehouse (1443) is the only remaining part of Rye House and is the earliest brick building in the county, standing on its moated site beside the River Lea. This was the scene of the infamous Rye House Plot in 1683.

A notable survivor in the much developed High Street in *Broxbourne* is the 1728 Monson Almshouse.

The church of St Augustine, situated by the New River, has an unusual second storey vestry in the north chapel, and a 12th century font of Purbeck marble.

Lea Valley Regional Park has one of its major centres here.

The old village of *Cheshunt* lies west of the A10, clustered adjacent to the flint church of St Mary. Grange cottages, Cheshunt Cottage with its bargeboards, hood-mouldings and neo-Elizabethan character, and a simple Georgian farmhouse form an attractive group in College Road.

The Dewhurst Charity School is a beautiful gabled and mullioned brick building dated 1640. The Old Parsonage is where Oliver Cromwell's son Richard died in 1712 after living quietly as 'Mr Clarke' for 30 years. Theobalds Park, the successor to Lord Burghley's Old Palace, was built in 1763, and has since been much altered, but in the grounds is the neglected Temple Bar designed by Christopher Wren, which is best approached along a lane from the New River.

At *Waltham Cross* the Eleanor Cross, erected by Edward I in 1291 along the route taken by his Queen's funeral cortège, still stands at the heart of the town, although greatly restored during the 19th century.

Anthony Trollope lived in Waltham Cross from 1859, where he wrote five of his best novels.

BROXBOURNE

DEWHURST CHARITY SCHOOL, CHESHUNT

POST OFFICE
CHEMIST

LITTLE BERKHAMSTEAD

◁ *HIGH STREET, HODDESDON*

LETTY GREEN: WELHAM GREEN: ESSENDON: LITTLE BERKHAMSTEAD: BROOKMANS PARK: POTTERS BAR

The water mill at *Letty Green* is an early 16th century timber-framed house with pargetting.

Woolmer's Park has a Doric collonade and an elegant avenue of limes.

Roxford is an early 18th century house with a bridge over the moat and a 16th century weatherboarded barn.

In 1784 the balloonist Vincent Lunardi touched down at *Welham Green* on the earliest flight over British soil, giving the name Balloon Corner to the junction of Dellsome, Parsonage and Huggins Lanes.

At *Essendon* the Cecil family of Hatfield House are featured in the heraldic crests on cottages, and in the name of the inn 'The Salisbury Crest'. Camfield Place, which Beatrix Potter visited as a child, is now the home of novelist Dame Barbara Cartland. Essendon Place is Regency, and the grounds are stocked with exotic trees and shrubs.

The village of *Little Berkhamstead* is located in a surprisingly hilly and wooded landscape south of Hertford, and is locked into a network of narrow country lanes. Opposite the mainly Victorian church of St Andrew is a row of weatherboarded cottages, and close by are Georgian Little Berkhamstead House, Danes and the Old Rectory. Folly Tower was erected in 1789 by John Stratton as an observatory, reputedly to monitor shipping movements on the Thames, although this would actually not have been possible.

Built partly on the grounds of Gobions, the former home of Sir Thomas More, where he wrote Utopia, *Brookmans Park* is a garden suburb of substantial homes built in the 1920s. The castellated brick arched entrance to the demolished Gobions was probably designed by James Gibb in 1730.

Potters Bar has now mushroomed into a town of 25,000 people. The old parts are restricted to a few inns and the medieval Wyllots Manor.

SOUTH MIMMS: BOREHAMWOOD: ELSTREE: RADLETT: SHENLEY: ALDENHAM

South Mimms is an oasis in a landscape dominated by the M25 and A100 junction. The remains of a motte and bailey castle lie about a mile to the north of the church, probably built in 1141AD by Geoffrey de Mandeville. A tiny village green is flanked by brick cottages, a Regency villa and Victorian almshouses. The church of St Giles, a medieval building restored by Street in 1878, stands on the nearby rise and boasts several brasses and monuments to the Frowyk family, who were successful London merchants.

The beautifully restored gateway to Dyrham Park is worth seeing and can be reached off the A1081 to Barnet.

North Mymms House is one of the best examples of late Elizabethan style in Hertfordshire, although sadly it is not open to the public. It was designed by Robert Lyminge the architect of Hatfield House.

St Mary's church is situated at the edge of North Mymms Park and has 13th century remains in the chancel, nave and aisles dated about 1340, and a 15th century tower. Several interesting monuments to priests and local families enrich the interior.

Once the centre of the British film industry, *Borehamwood* studios are now faded and shabby remnants of more glorious days.

The small village of *Elstree* on Watling Street lies partly in Greater London and has a Victorian church and the medieval Hollybush Inn. The Leys, a house in Barnet Lane by George Walton, friend of Charles Rennie Mackintosh, belongs to the Glasgow Art Nouveau School of design. Haberdashers' Aske's School, once Aldenham House and built in 1700, and Home Farm by Butterfield lie in parkland to the north west.

NORTH MYMMS PARK GATES

The former Handley Page aerodrome buildings are on *Radlett* aerodrome. Skybreak House is a single storey 1966 house by Foster Associates, which steps down a north facing slope, utilising an inclined glass wall to encourage maximum solar gain.

St Botolph's church at *Shenley* was begun in the 15th century. The architect, Sir Nicholas Hawksmoor, lived in the parish and was buried there in 1736.

Standing just off the Watford to Radlett road is *Aldenham*, a pleasant village composed of cottages and old black barns, and a large church with a small spire on its west tower, and elements of Norman, early English, Decorated and Perpendicular architecture. Aldenham School was founded in 1596.

A reserve at Hillfield has become a refuge for wildfowl in winter. Aldenham reservoir was dug in 1795 to replenish the Colne river, which was itself used by the canal, and a country park is now established at the north end of the water.

VILLAGE POND, SHENLEY

ALDENHAM

ST JAMES'S CHURCHYARD, STANSTEAD ABBOTTS

STANSTEAD ABBOTTS: WORMLEY: GOFF'S OAK: CUFFLEY

The Clockhouse stands at the head of *Stanstead Abbotts'* High Street, close to the gabled Red Lion Inn. Stanstead Hall is Georgian and has an unusual circular stair turret. The redundant church of St James lies apart, and has a brick chapel dated 1577, a picturesque timber porch, Georgian box-pews and a three-decker pulpit in its whitewashed interior.

At *Wormley*, the mansion of Wormleybury, designed by Robert Mylne in 1767, had a gigantic stone portico added in 1782, and the interiors are by Robert Adam. The stable block has a fine clock turret. The church of St Lawrence has a Norman north doorway, and an unusual Norman font, decorated with a frieze of leaves and cable mouldings.

The village of *Goff's Oak* is notable only for its bizarre medieval revivalist buildings at Colesgrove Manor, built in the early 19th century, with toy-like lodge houses decorated by barge-boards, lattice windows and dormer dovecotes.

The commuter village of *Cuffley* centred around the railway station is the home of the Great Wood Country Park, which stretches around in a giant horseshoe to the village of Northaw.

THE RED LION AND THE CLOCKHOUSE, STANSTEAD ABBOTTS

THE CHILTERNS AND DACORUM

Stretching out into Buckinghamshire the spur of land called Dacorum embraces part of the Chilterns and the Gade Valley, and contains the historic towns of Hemel Hempstead, Berkhamsted and Tring. In the woodlands of Ashridge Hertfordshire reaches its highest point, and this is where the greatest physical contrasts are experienced.

The picturesque villages of Aldbury, Little Gaddesden and Sarratt make the most of their contrasting locations, either in the valley or on the ridge.

The valley is further enhanced by the Grand Union Canal as it wends its way north-westwards to the Midlands, and produces a rich legacy of industrial architecture in bridges, locks and related engineering structures.

Of the country houses in the Chiltern Spur, prominent amongst them are Ashridge Park, Tring Park, Champneys and Stocks at Aldbury, and there are exceptional medieval churches at Hemel Hempstead, an essentially Norman construction, and at Sarratt.

LITTLE GADDESDEN CHURCH

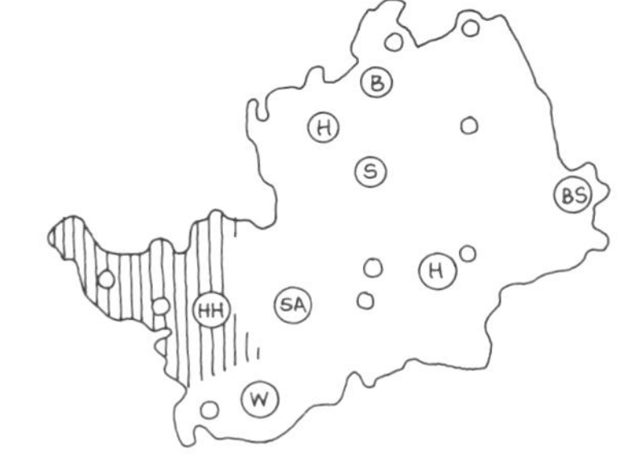

BERKHAMSTED: NORTHCHURCH

William the Conquerer accepted the Crown of England from Saxon nobles in *Berkhamsted* and about 1150AD the castle was built, of which only the motte and bailey remain.

The town is linear, strung out for nearly a mile along a prepossessing High Street which follows the line of the River Bulbourne. The Grand Union Canal runs alongside the river and the parallel railway cuts off the town from its castle site.

Berkhamsted School was founded in 1541 and the original building stands in Castle Street, a long brick-built room with kingpost roof.

Incent's House is of the 16th century and is a fine half-timbered building with overhanging upper floor. Although much restored by Butterfield in 1870-71 for use as a Sunday School, the 16th century Court House has a well preserved timber frame.

The High Street is packed with interesting dwellings, the Victorian Old Town Hall and Market House of 1859, the Sayer Almshouses of 1684, and 17th and 18th century inns.

The massive church of St Peter, built of flint stone, has been modified many times over the centuries since its 12th century foundation and has a memorial window to William Cowper the poet, who was born here in 1731 when his father was rector. On the steep slopes to the south of the High Street are many Victorian and Edwardian villas set in mature gardens.

Northchurch was once a separate village, but is now joined with Berkhamsted. The church of St Mary has a Totternhoe stone crossing tower, and the remainder of the structure is of flint. Grim's Dyke is an ancient ditch measuring 35 feet across.

BERKHAMSTED MARKET HOUSE

BERKHAMSTED CASTLE RUINS

GRAND UNION CANAL LOCKS, BERKHAMSTED

NAVE DETAIL, ST MARY'S CHURCH, HEMEL HEMPSTEAD

HEMEL HEMPSTEAD: KING'S LANGLEY

The Norman church of St Mary at *Hemel Hempstead* is the finest in the county, a large cruciform building of flint rubble and Roman bricks, started in 1140AD and added to in later centuries. The nave, aisles, transepts, crossing tower and chancel are all Norman with arcades of carved billet and zigzag arches and capitals. The chancel is the earliest part and is rib-vaulted, a rare feature in England. The 1175AD nave has six bays with circular piers whose capitals are decorated in a variety of ornamented scalloping. The clerestory is also Norman and is an extremely rare feature.

The crossing tower is crowned by a sixty metre high leaded spire. The old town centre is now submerged in a sea of new town housing which makes Hemel Hempstead the third largest in Hertfordshire, but fortunately the old town is on a ridge which overlooks the meadows of the River Gade and retains views of the Chiltern Hills beyond.

The High Street rises along the edge of the hillside and opens out to the church at the half-way point. Notable individual buildings are Lloyds Bank (1884) in terracotta, the White Hart, a timber framed inn, and the Kings Arms, another half-timbered structure. Early 18th century town houses are plentiful, and the old Town Hall, built in 1851, is a neo-Jacobean curiosity in red brick with stone dressings. Townsend House was probably a medieval hall-house and has a timber frame with a gabled and jettied cross wing. Alleyways and lanes slope eastwards off the High Street creating an intimate feel to this part of the town.

At Piccott's End, a row of timber-framed gabled cottages, one of which contains important medieval wall paintings (1500) discovered in 1953 and which are open for viewing to the public. Piccott's End Farm, and Piccott's End Mill and Mill House are further charming examples of vernacular timber-framed, weatherboarded and red brick building of the area.

To the west of the church Gadebridge Park has a 16th century stone porch called Charter Tower as a doorway to a formal garden beyond.

The new town plan was prepared by G. A. Jellicoe in 1947.

At *King's Langley* the remains of the Dominican Priory now forms part of a school. The Rose and Crown is of chequered brickwork and has a fine Regency verandah. The church of All Saints has the tomb chest of Edmund of Langley, the fifth son of Edward III, which is decorated with 13 alabaster heraldic shields.

HIGH STREET, HEMEL HEMPSTEAD

TRING: WIGGINTON: LONG MARSTON: PUTTENHAM

An ancient town built close to the crossing of the Icknield Way and Roman Akeman Street, *Tring* is in the most westerly part of Hertfordshire in the lee of the Chilterns. The Grand Union Canal was an important link with the outside world and brought this formerly isolated agricultural settlement to life in the early 19th century, and saw the building of wharves, a mill, reservoirs, and housing to accommodate incoming workers.

Tring Park Mansion was built in the time of Charles II and is attributed to Christopher Wren, but this was masked by a late 19th century exterior added by the first Lord Rothschild who bought the house in 1873. The parkland is now divided by the town bypass, but nevertheless stretches attractively up into the Chilterns behind Wigginton.

The main street exudes late Victoriana and side streets contain an interesting blend of alleys, courts and back lanes.

Situated high up on a spur of the Chilterns above Tring, *Wigginton* looks across to Ashridge and the Bridgwater Monument beyond Aldbury, and has views over Buckinghamshire to the west. Below the road, river and canal wind up the valley.

St Bartholomew's church is a restored late medieval building. On the edge of Tring Park, which now adheres to Wigginton because of the division caused by the A41 motorway, is a ruined 18th century summer house in Greek Temple style, and an obelisk to the memory of a former guest of King Charles II at Tring Park, Nell Gwynne.

Long Marston straggles around a crossroads in watery flatlands in the extreme west of the county. The 15th century tower is all that remains of a deserted medieval church, some fragments of which have been incorporated into a late Victorian replacement.

In 1751 the village pond was the scene of England's last witch-lynching when Ruth Osborn was captured and drowned by 'ducking'.

A tiny hamlet close to Long Marston, *Puttenham*, has a remarkable church with a glorious 15th century nave roof, with moulded beams enriched with bosses of flowers and shields, angels on the ends and eight standing figures of saints beneath. A plaque on one wall recalls that all 15 men who went to the 1914-18 war returned safely and offers thanks to God.

BREWERY CARRIAGEWAY, TRING

LONG MARSTON COTTAGE

ALDBURY: LITTLE GADDESDEN: GREAT GADDESDEN: NETTLEDON: POTTEN END:

Nestling in the valley below Ashridge, half-timbered houses cluster around picturesque *Aldbury* village green, with its pond and old wooden stocks, and nearby the elegant church tower rises above the trees. The Pendley Chapel inside the church is separated from the south aisle by an original Perpendicular stone screen with castellated top.

High on the hillside overlooking the village stands a monument to the 3rd Duke of Bridgewater who lived at nearby Ashridge, and was dubbed the 'Father of Inland Navigation' or 'The Canal Duke'. In the early 19th century Aldbury was a centre for straw plaiting and supplied to the hat-making industry in Luton.

STOCKS FARM, ALDBURY

Little Gaddesden is strung out along a ridge top route in the Chilterns, a continuous series of greens flanked by farms, cottages and substantial houses, and punctuated by memorial stones.

John of Gaddesden's house is a splendid timber-framed building with overhanging pargetted upper floor dating from the 15th century, and replacing the original house erected by John of Gaddesden, who died in 1361, having been Court Physician to Kings Edward II and III.

The Manor House, dated 1576, has stepped gables and stands behind thick yew hedges.

Ashridge is a vast Gothic revival mansion built by James Wyatt in 1808 and added to by his nephew Jeffry Wyatville between 1814 and 1820. However, the house began its existence as the English College of Bonhommes founded in 1283, and Princess Elizabeth lived here during the reign of Mary, before the house passed to Sir Thomas Egerton in 1604, whose descendants remained there until soon after the end of the First World War. The gardens and park were landscaped by Capability Brown in about 1760 and by Repton in the early 19th century. Ashridge is now a Management College.

The Church of St Peter and St Paul lies apart from the village, overlooking magnificent countryside from its high vantage point on the edge of the northern escarpment of the Chilterns.

The River Gade passes *Great Gaddesden* in a necklace of ponds and water meadows linking to Water End. The village itself is undistinguished, but the church of St John the Baptist has 12th century chancel walls and monuments to the Halsey family. Gaddesden Hall, built for the Halseys by James Wyatt between 1768 and 1773, stands high above the river, which has been widened here to form a very attractive lake.

A tiny settlement in the Chilterns, *Nettleden* has some 17th century cottages and a small brick church with a flint tower. In the early 19th century the Duke of Bridgewater had a flint and brick-faced cutting built through the hill behind the village which leads to Frithsden, and a brick bridge carries an avenue across it to Ashridge.

The pond and pub on the village green at *Potten End* make a pleasant traditional picture in this largely modern Chiltern village. Iron Age Grim's Dyke starts immediately to the west.

◁ *VILLAGE POND, ALDBURY*

GREAT GADDESDEN

ASHRIDGE

LITTLE GADDESDEN MANOR

RENTSTREET BARNS, BOVINGDON

FLAMSTEAD: BOVINGDON: SARRATT: FLAUNDEN: CHIPPERFIELD

The church of St Leonard at *Flamstead* has an important series of wall paintings which were discovered in 1930; in the nave the lower parts of four apostles of the 13th century, and a large figure of St Christopher of the 15th century. Above the chancel arch and in the north east chapel are Doomsday scenes and a series of the Passion depicting the Betrayal, the Last Supper, the Crucifixion, the Mocking of Christ, the Entombment, the Crowning with Thorns and the Resurrection. The clock beneath the window of the bell chamber has the figure of Father Time proclaiming 'Time Flies' and 'Mind Your Business'.

The hilltop village is built around the church, and comprises brick and pargetted cottages and 'The Star Inn'.

At *Bovingdon* Rentstreet Barns on the Chipperfield road are 16th and 17th century.

The extraordinary Holy Cross church of *Sarratt* has a cruciform plan and is built of flint, pudding stone and bricks. The saddleback tower is unusual in Hertfordshire.

The village stretches along a broad undulating green with loosely scattered dwellings and inns on both sides, culminating at the southern end in a village pond and The Cricketer's Arms.

The crumbling walls of *Flaunden* church lie amongst the nettles at Flaunden Bottom on the River Chess, but the new church is the first designed by Giles Gilbert Scott in 1838 and incorporates fragments of the old church.

An inn, a church and some brick cottages face onto a small square green cut out of the woodlands at *Chipperfield*. The Common is a delightful feature of the village.

◁ *CHILTERNS LANDSCAPE*

FLAMSTEAD VILLAGE

SARRATT VILLAGE GREEN ▷

SARRATT CHURCH

WATFORD AND THE SOUTH

Watford is the largest town in Hertfordshire and has suffered badly from the scramble for commercial space resulting from its proximity to London and its location on the M1 and main railway line. The historic core of this old country town has been largely submerged by brash new developments since the Second World War. However, despite the growing pressures on Hertsmere, the villages of Bedmond and Oxhey remain relatively unaffected, and even in Rickmansworth, Chorley Wood and Croxley Green it is possible to find quiet backwaters which retain vestiges of former times.

The pleasant upper reaches of the River Chess and the green fields surrounding these towns provide welcome open countryside, within easy reach, and the M25 now takes some of the traffic strain which this whole area has suffered from in recent years.

CASSIOBURY PARK, WATFORD

WATFORD: BUSHEY

Watford is the largest town in Hertfordshire, and stands on the main line railway into Euston, alongside both the M1 and M25 motorways and at the end of the London Underground system. In places it has the character of a London suburb but retains vestiges of the old town centred upon the church and the High Street, wending its way down to the River Colne.

The church of St Mary with its flint tower topped by Hertfordshire spike, bristles boldly amongst the surrounding high rise buildings and ponderous multi-storey car parks. New developments have unfortunately all but obliterated the timber-framed High Street of recent times, and only a few noteworthy buildings have survived, amongst them Elizabeth Fuller's Free School (1704) and the Bedford Almshouses founded in 1580, both flanking the churchyard. Watford Museum is housed in the Georgian former offices of Benskin's Brewery. Remnants of 15th and 16th century timber-framed buildings between nos. 156 and 195 High Street, highlight the loss of Watford's late medieval heritage.

In Cassiobury Park, site of the mansion of the Earls of Essex, stands the 18th century brick Dower House, a fine classical dwelling.

The Grand Union Canal towpath leads to Grove Mill by the river and an elegant balustraded bridge dated 1800 spans the canal carrying the driveway to the Grove, former home of the Earl of Clarendon, and a predominantly 18th century building.

ST MARY'S CHURCH, WATFORD

Holy Rood in Market Street is a Roman Catholic church designed by J. F. Bentley in 1883-90 and is a masterpiece of Gothic Revival architecture. Bentley later designed Westminster Cathedral.

A leafy suburban neighbour of Watford, *Bushey* has a 13th century church, a village pond and some quaint pargetted cottages, but is principally made up of opulent villas of Regency, Victorian and Edwardian periods, and was once the home of many artists. Hubert von Herkomer, a Bavarian artist, settled in Bushey in 1873 and founded an Art School. The only remaining fragment of his own house stands in Melbourne Road which was named 'Lululaund' after his wife and was designed by the famous American architect H. H. Richardson.

THE FORMER ELIZABETH FULLER FREE SCHOOL, WATFORD

BEDFORD ALMSHOUSES, WATFORD

HIGH STREET SHOP, WATFORD

RICKMANSWORTH

The arrival of the Metropolitan Railway in 1887 transformed this small settlement on the banks of the River Colne into an attractive residential town, and during the 1930's *Rickmansworth* expanded dramatically.

Because of its watery site at the conjunction of the Chess and Colne the old part of Rickmansworth has an open meadowy edge, albeit encroached upon by railway and industrial paraphernalia. Church Street alone retains small country-town character, and around the church are some interesting buildings, notably the Bury, an early 17th century brick and timber-framed house, and the Priory, now used as Council Offices, which was built in 1740 and stands on the site of a house in which William Penn, founder of Pennsylvania, once lived. The Old Vicarage was altered frequently during the 18th and 19th centuries but has a core of late medieval timber framing and an overhanging oriel on the first floor.

The canal produced functional Stockers House and Lock Cottage, and nearby is an attractive group of buildings at Stockers Farm House.

Moor Park is a splendid 18th century mansion situated in parkland about a mile from the Town centre, and represents a remodelling by Thornhill and Leoni of the great 17th century house built by the Duke of Monmouth. Cased in Portland Stone, it has a four column portico at the entrance in Corinthian order. Inside the best features are the full height entrance hall with gallery, painted walls, a painted saloon ceiling, and a ballroom decorated by Robert Adam. The park was remodelled by Capability Brown between 1755 and 1760 and a tea pavilion by Adam survived as a dwelling north of the house. The Duchess of Monmouth ordered the 'beheading' of the oak trees in the park in mourning for the Duke's death in 1685. Moor Park is now a Golf Club and the house is occasionally open for viewing.

MOOR PARK, RICKMANSWORTH

THE INN AND THE CHURCH, RICKMANSWORTH ▷

CANAL LOCKS, RICKMANSWORTH

FORMER OVALTINE MODEL DAIRY, ABBOTS LANGLEY

ABBOTS LANGLEY: BEDMOND: CHORLEYWOOD: CROXLEY GREEN: OXHEY: EASTBURY

Encircled by motorways and dual carriage-ways the suburban community of *Abbots Langley* slopes down to the River Gade from the original village centre where the church of St Lawrence stands. Norman arcades of zig-zags and billets resemble those at Hemel Hempstead and together with the Decorated south chancel chapel make the church exceptionally interesting.

The Ovaltine Model Dairy was built in 1931 and forms a rustic collection of thatched, half-timbered and tiled buildings now converted into flats and houses.

The tiny village of *Bedmond* was the birth-place of Nicholas Breakspear in 1100AD, the only Englishman ever to become Pope.

Significant for its large common, *Chorleywood* is a typical 'between the wars' suburban settlement. Voysey built himself 'The Orchard' here in 1900, and neighbouring 'Sunnybank' in 1903-4. Heronsgate was founded by Feargus O'Connor's Co-operative Land Company in 1847, and planned with a school and 35 cottages on plots of between two and four acres in an attempt to encourage a back-to-the-land community.

Sandwiched between Watford and Rickmans-worth, *Croxley Green* still has a large green surrounded by several pretty buildings. Between the railway and the River Gade is Croxley Hall Farm with its beautiful late medieval tithe barn (1400) recently restored by the County Council. It measures 101 feet by 40 feet and has a nave and aisles, one entrance transept and a crownpost roof.

The chapel at *Oxhey* was built in 1612 by Sir James Altham and restored during the 19th century, but the rest of the village has mostly been absorbed into Bushey.

Situated in *Eastbury* is the Glade, a house most probably designed by Voysey, and displaying his characteristic sloping buttresses and stone surrounds to the windows set in rough-cast walls.

ST LAWRENCE CHURCH, ABBOTS LANGLEY

BIBLIOGRAPHY

The Buildings of England: Hertfordshire: Nikolaus Pevsner and Bridget Cherry: Penguin
A Pictorial Guide to Hertfordshire: Eric Meadows: White Crescent Press Ltd
Hertfordshire: R. M. Healey: Faber and Faber

GREEN TYE COTTAGE

PLACES OPEN TO THE PUBLIC

NGS: National Gardens Scheme

AYOT ST LAWRENCE	Shaw's Corner	National Trust
BENINGTON	The Lordship	The Gardens
FURNEUX PELHAM	Furneux Pelham Hall	The Gardens (NGS)
GREAT MUNDEN	Great Munden House	The Gardens (NGS)
HATFIELD	Hatfield House	House and Gardens
KNEBWORTH	Knebworth House	House and Gardens
LITTLE GADDESDEN	Ashridge	The Gardens
LITTLE GADDESDEN	Ashridge Woods	National Trust
POTTERS BAR	Wrotham Park	The Gardens (NGS)
RICKMANSWORTH	Moor Park Mansion	House and Park
SARRATT	Great Sarratt Hall	The Gardens (NGS)
ST ALBANS	Gorhambury	House and Gardens
ST PAULS WALDEN	St Pauls Waldenbury	The Gardens (for charity)
WARE	Scott's Grotto	The Gardens
WATTON-AT-STONE	Woodhall Park	House open by appointment

Other places open to the public but not mentioned in text

(National Gardens Scheme, Red Cross and other charities)

Abbots House, Abbots Langley
Manor House, Ayot St Lawrence
Odsey Park, Baldock
Cokenash, Barkway
Hopleys, Bishops Stortford
Hipkins, Broxbourne
Capel Manor
Waterdell House, Croxley Green
Holwell Manor, Essendon

West Lodge Park, Hadley Wood
12 High Cross Road, Hemel Hempstead
Danes, Little Berkhamstead
Burloes, Royston
Gardens of the Rose, St Albans
Hill House, Stanstead Abbots
The Dell, Wheathampstead
Lamer Hill, Wheathampstead
Lamer Lodge, Wheathampstead

For further details see 'Historic Houses, Castles and Gardens', published annually

INDEX

Numbers in italics indicate illustrations

HARE STREET, OAK AND ELM COTTAGES

Books Published by THE BOOK CASTLE

CHANGES IN OUR LANDSCAPE: Aspects of Bedfordshire, Buckinghamshire and the Chilterns 1947-1992: Eric Meadows. Over 350 photographs from the author's collection spanning nearly 50 years.

COUNTRYSIDE CYCLING IN BEDFORDSHIRE, BUCKINGHAMSHIRE AND HERTFORDSHIRE: Mick Payne. Twenty rides on and off-road for all the family.

PUB WALKS FROM COUNTRY STATIONS: Bedfordshire and Hertfordshire: Clive Higgs. Fourteen circular country rambles, each starting and finishing at a railway station and incorporating a pub stop at a mid way point.

PUB WALKS FROM COUNTRY STATIONS: Buckinghamshire and Oxfordshire: Clive Higgs. Circular rambles incorporating pub-stops.

LOCAL WALKS: South Bedfordshire and North Chilterns: Vaughan Basham. Twenty-seven thematic circular walks.

LOCAL WALKS: North and Mid Bedfordshire: Vaughan Basham. Twenty-five thematic circular walks.

FAMILY WALKS: Chilterns South: Nick Moon. Thirty 3 to 5 mile circular walks.

FAMILY WALKS: Chilterns North: Nick Moon. Thirty shorter circular walks.

CHILTERN WALKS: Hertfordshire, Bedfordshire and North Bucks: Nick Moon.

CHILTERN WALKS: Buckinghamshire: Nick Moon.

CHILTERN WALKS: Oxfordshire and West Buckinghamshire: Nick Moon. A trilogy of circular walks, in association with the Chiltern Society. Each volume contains 30 circular walks.

OXFORDSHIRE WALKS: Oxford, the Cotswolds and the Cherwell Valley: Nick Moon.

OXFORDSHIRE WALKS: Oxford, the Downs and the Thames Valley: Nick Moon. Two volumes that complement Chiltern Walks: Oxfordshire, and complete coverage of the county, in association with the Oxford Fieldpaths Society. Thirty circular walks in each.

THE D'ARCY DALTON WAY: Nick Moon. Long-distance footpath across the Oxfordshire Cotswolds and Thames Valley, with various circular walk suggestions.

THE CHILTERN WAY: Nick Moon. A guide to the new 133 mile circular Long-Distance Path through Bedfordshire, Buckinghamshire, Hertfordshire and Oxfordshire, as planned by the Chiltern Society.

JOURNEYS INTO BEDFORDSHIRE: Anthony Mackay. Foreword by The Marquess of Tavistock, Woburn Abbey. A lavish book of over 150 evocative ink drawings.

COCKNEY KID & COUNTRYMEN: Ted Enever. The Second World War remembered by the children of Woburn Sands and Aspley Guise. A six year old boy is evacuated from London's East End to start life in a Buckinghamshire village.

BUCKINGHAM AT WAR: Pip Brimson. Stories of courage, humour and pathos as Buckingham people adapt to war.

WINGS OVER WING: The Story of a World War II Bomber Training Unit: Mike Warth. The activities of RAF Wing in Buckinghamshire.

JOURNEYS INTO BUCKINGHAMSHIRE: Anthony Mackay. Superb line drawings plus background text: large format landscape gift book.

BUCKINGHAMSHIRE MURDERS: Len Woodley. Nearly two centuries of nasty crimes.

WINGRAVE: A Rothschild Village in the Vale: Margaret and Ken Morley. Thoroughly researched and copiously illustrated survey of the last 200 years in this lovely village between Aylesbury and Leighton Buzzard.

HISTORIC FIGURES IN THE BUCKINGHAMSHIRE LANDSCAPE: John Houghton. Major personalities and events that have shaped the county's past, including Bletchley Park.

TWICE UPON A TIME: John Houghton. North Bucks short stories loosely based on fact.

SANCTITY AND SCANDAL IN BEDS AND BUCKS: John Houghton. A miscellany of unholy people and events.

MANORS and MAYHEM, PAUPERS and PARSONS: Tales from Four Shires: Beds., Bucks., Herts. and Northants: John Houghton. Little known historical snippets and stories.

THE LAST PATROL: Len Woodley. Policemen killed on duty while serving the Thames Valley.

FOLK: Characters and Events in the History of Bedfordshire and Northamptonshire: Vivienne Evans. Anthology of people of yesteryear arranged alphabetically by village or town.

JOHN BUNYAN: His Life and Times: Vivienne Evans. Highly praised and readable account.

THE RAILWAY AGE IN BEDFORDSHIRE: Fred Cockman. Classic, illustrated account of early railway history.

A LASTING IMPRESSION: Michael Dundrow. A boyhood evacuee recalls his years in the Chiltern village of Totternhoe near Dunstable.

GLEANINGS REVISITED: Nostalgic Thoughts of a Bedfordshire Farmer's Boy: E.W. O'Dell. His own sketches and early photographs adorn this lively account of rural Bedfordshire in days gone by.

BEDFORDSHIRE'S YESTERYEARS Vol 2: The Rural Scene: Brenda Fraser Newstead. Vivid first-hand accounts of country life two or three generations ago.

BEDFORDSHIRE'S YESTERYEARS Vol 3: Craftsmen and Tradespeople: Brenda Fraser-Newstead. Fascinating recollections over several generations practising many vanishing crafts and trades.

BEDFORDSHIRE'S YESTERYEARS Vol 4: War Times and Civil Matters: Brenda Fraser-Newstead. Two World Wars, plus transport, law and order, etc.

DUNNO'S ORIGINALS: A facsimile of the rare pre-Victorian history of Dunstable and surrounding villages. New preface and glossary by John Buckledee, Editor of The Dunstable Gazette.

PROUD HERITAGE: A Brief History of Dunstable, 1000-2000AD: Vivienne Evans. Century by century account of the town's rich tradition and key events, many of national significance.

DUNSTABLE WITH THE PRIORY: 1100-1550: Vivienne Evans. Dramatic growth of Henry I's important new town around a major crossroads.

DUNSTABLE IN TRANSITION: 1550-1700: Vivienne Evans. Wealth of original material as the town evolves without the Priory.

OLD DUNSTABLE: Bill Twaddle. A new edition of this collection of early photographs.

BOURNE and BRED: A Dunstable Boyhood Between the Wars: Colin Bourne. An elegantly written, well illustrated book capturing the spirit of the town over fifty years ago.

OLD HOUGHTON: Pat Lovering. Pictorial record capturing the changing appearances of Houghton Regis over the past 100 years.

ROYAL HOUGHTON: Pat Lovering. Illustrated history of Houghton Regis from the earliest of times to the present.

GIRLS IN BLUE: Christine Turner. The activities of the famous Luton Girls Choir properly documented over its 41 year period from 1936 to 1977.

THE STOPSLEY BOOK: James Dyer. Definitive, detailed account of this historic area of Luton. 150 rare photographs.

THE STOPSLEY PICTURE BOOK: James Dyer. New material and photographs make an ideal companion to The Stopsley Book.

PUBS and PINTS: The Story of Luton's Public Houses and Breweries: Stuart Smith. The background to beer in the town, plus hundreds of photographs, old and new.

LUTON AT WAR - VOLUME ONE: As compiled by the Luton News in 1947, a well illustrated thematic account.

LUTON AT WAR - VOLUME TWO: Second part of the book compiled by The Luton News, with a new index by James Dyer.

THE CHANGING FACE OF LUTON: An Illustrated History: Stephen Bunker, Robin Holgate and Marian Nichols. Luton's development from earliest times to the present busy industrial town. Illustrated in colour and mono.

WHERE THEY BURNT THE TOWN HALL DOWN: Luton, the First World War and the Peace Day Riots, July 1919: Dave Craddock. Detailed analysis of a notorious incident.

THE MEN WHO WORE STRAW HELMETS: Policing Luton, 1841974: Tom Madigan. Fine chronicled history, many rare photographs; author served in Luton Police for fifty years.

BETWEEN THE HILLS: The Story of Lilley, a Chiltern Village: Roy Pinnock. A priceless piece of our heritage - the rural beauty remains but the customs and way of life described here have largely disappeared.

JOURNEYS INTO BEDFORDSHIRE
AND
JOURNEYS INTO BUCKINGHAMSHIRE

by Anthony Mackay

These two books of ink drawings reveal an intriguing historic heritage and capture the spirit of England's rural heartland, ranging widely over cottages and stately homes, over bridges, churches and mills, over sandy woods, chalk downs and watery river valleys.

Every corner of Bedfordshire and Buckinghamshire has been explored in the search for material, and although the choice of subjects is essentially a personal one, the resulting collection represents a unique record of the environment today.

The notes and maps, which accompany the drawings, lend depth to the books, and will assist others on their own journeys around the counties.

Anthony Mackay's pen-and-ink drawings are of outstanding quality and are better able to show both depth and detail than any photograph.

CHANGES IN OUR LANDSCAPE:

Aspects of Bedfordshire, Buckinghamshire and the Chilterns 1947-1992

by Eric Meadows

In the post-War years, this once quiet rural backwater between Oxford and Cambridge has undergone growth and change – and the expert camera of Eric Meadows has captured it all...

An enormous variety of landscape, natural and man-made, from yesteryear and today – open downs and rolling farmland, woods and commons, ancient earthworks, lakes and moats, vanished elms.

Quarries, nature reserves and landscape gardens. Many building styles- churches of all periods, stately homes and town dwellings, rural pubs, gatehouses and bridges. Secluded villages contrast their timeless lifestyle with the bustle of modern developing towns and their industries.

Distilled from a huge collection of 25,000 photographs, this book offers the author's personal selection of over 350 that best display the area's most attractive features and its notable changes over 50 years. The author's detailed captions and notes complete a valuable local history. The original hardback edition was in print for only 4 weeks in 1992. By popular demand now in a large format paperback.

THE HILL OF THE MARTYR

An Architectural History of St. Albans Abbey

by Eileen Roberts

This popular but scholarly handbook covers the whole sweep of development from the martyrdom of Alban to the modern shrine restoration. It describes and explains each feature - from the Saxon Benedictine monastery, via the great Romanesque church of the Normans, through medieval growth and change, then from near ruin to Victorian salvation and twentieth century glory. Its one hundred specially prepared pictures, plans and diagrams add a further dimension to our understanding and enjoyment.

Over twelve centuries after the monastery's foundation, the present building fulfils an invaluable role as cathedral for Hertfordshire and Bedfordshire.